MINGMING II

& the Impossible Voyage

ROGER D. TAYLOR

MINGMING II

& the Impossible Voyage

*With illustrations
from the author's log-book*

𝔉

THE FITZROY PRESS

Published by The FitzRoy Press 2020.

F
The FitzRoy Press
5 Regent Gate
Waltham Cross
Herts EN8 7AF

ISBN 978 0955803 581

A catalogue record for this book is available from the British Library

Publishing management by Troubador Publishing Ltd, Leicestershire, UK
Printed and bound in the UK by TJ International, Padstow, Cornwall

MIX
Paper from
responsible sources
FSC
www.fsc.org   FSC® C013056

An thog thu rithist an seòl mór a ghlacas a'ghaoth shiabach...?
Somhairle MacGill-Eain, *An Saothach*

Will you raise again the big sail that will catch the sweeping wind...?
Sorley MacLean, *The Ship*

CONTENTS

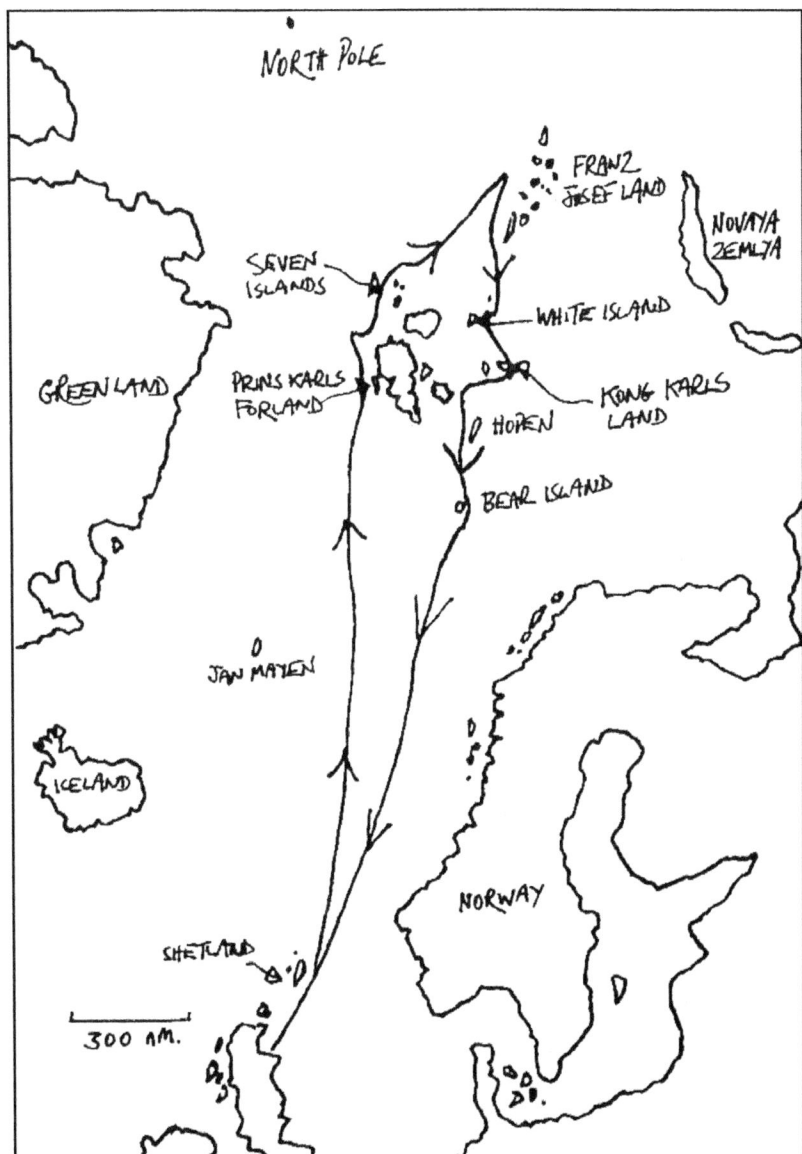

Mingming II's 2018 Voyage

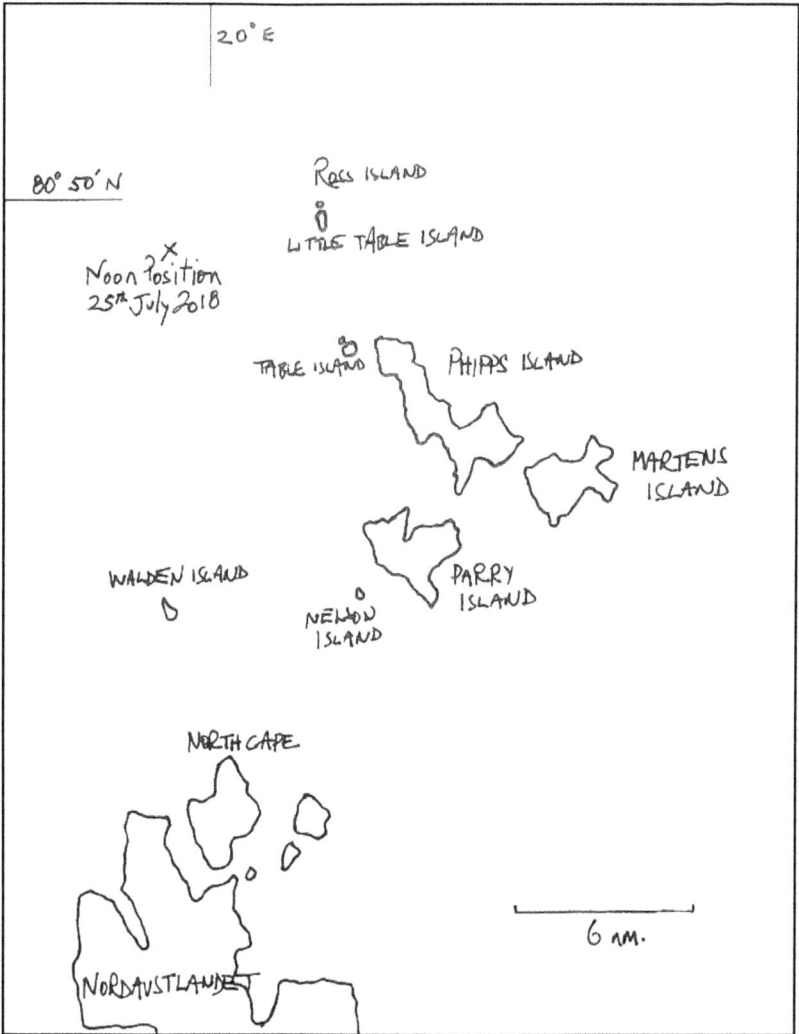

80° 50′ N

20° E

Noon Position
25ᵗʰ July 2018

Ross Island

Little Table Island

Table Island   Phipps Island

Martens Island

Walden Island

Parry Island

Nelson Island

North Cape

6 nm.

Nordaustlandet

The Seven Islands

The islands of north-west Franz Josef Land

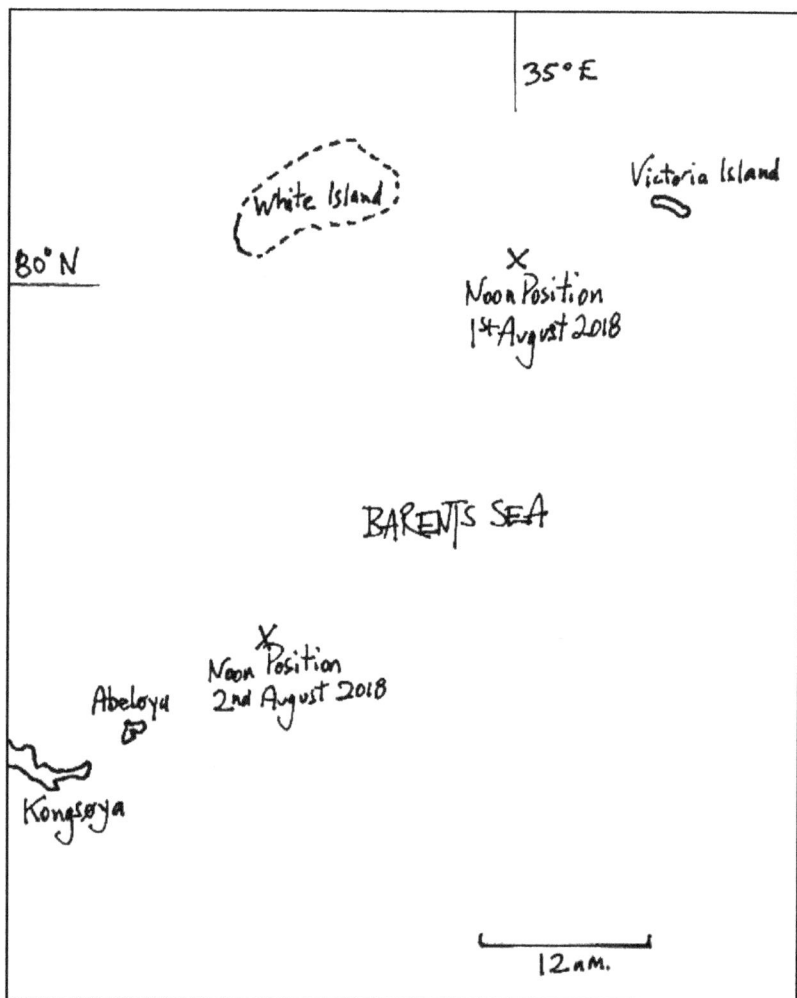

35° E

White Island

Victoria Island

80° N

X
Noon Position
1st August 2018

BARENTS SEA

X
Noon Position
2nd August 2018

Abeløya

Kongsøya

12 n.M.

From White Island and Victoria Island to the east end of Kong Karls Land

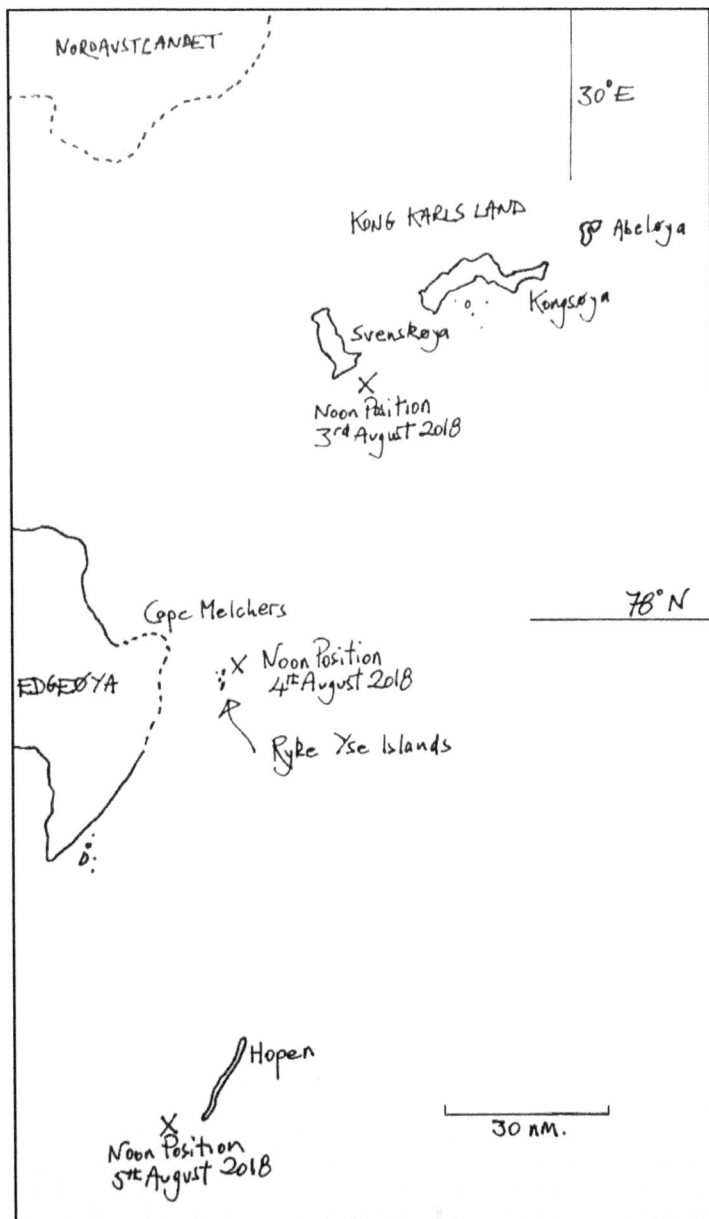

NORDAUSTLANDET

30°E

KONG KARLS LAND

&P Abeløya

Kongsøya

Svenskøya

X
Noon Position
3rd August 2018

Cape Melchers

78°N

;X Noon Position
4th August 2018

EDGEØYA

Ryke Yse Islands

Ò:

Hopen

X
Noon Position
5th August 2018

30 nm.

From Kong Karls Land to Hopen

xiii

PROLOGUE

I do not believe in gods or afterlives; there is mystery, without doubt, but no magic. Once I am dead the decomposing constituents of my body, my only self, will be reabsorbed into the fabric of the worldly matter from which they came; no more, no less. This is a pleasing thought: to give something back after taking so much; to be reallocated randomly across the animate and the inanimate; to merge into the tail feather of a siskin, the leaf of a mountain ash, the eye, perhaps, of a blue whale; to wash down into the deep sea and reanimate the maternal fluid. All is possible.

To go to the wild places is to come nearer to that redistribution which is the cycle of life. To taste the solitude of a distant sea is to embrace the collectivity of all things. It is a negation of the ego, an underscoring of a pure and beautiful insignificance. It is a kind of rebirth, a cleansing of the warped, the cynical and the confused.

That is why, from time to time, I must go; and why, each time, I must push a little harder, a little further. Perhaps one day I will reach the very core of what I seek, although I doubt it; a perfect and certain understanding is too elusive to grasp. There have been moments when I have felt the tips of my fingers close gently around it, only to find it gone. All that remains is a faint and indeterminate scent, the memory of a gossamer touch, a distant reverberation as of placid waves on a far shore.

Such a delicate enlightenment cannot be coaxed out of the teeming conurbations. I have searched for it on high and distant mountains given only to the sough of the wind and the raven's croak, but even there a proximate mankind weighs too heavily on the mind and the senses. Only the far seas and the icy islands clothed in an unwavering inhospitality seem able to provide the pure and magnificent indifference against which a man can measure his existence.

Time and distance are the great cleansers. They scour the mind to a crystal clarity as thoroughly as the relentless wash of wind and wave leave a tiny yacht's decks unblemished and sparkling. That is why a voyage must be long and unbroken. Forty days alone in the wilderness is a minimum; sixty or seventy the ideal. Longer than that would require a vessel surpassing the minimal, to the detriment of the enterprise: to achieve true absorption into them, the wild places should be approached by insinuation rather than by assault. They will cede, sometimes, to humility, but will close ranks against the brash, the aggressive, the pretentious and the unseeing.

The lonelier the target, the less known, the less frequented, the more difficult of access, the better. The aim is not simply to reach and taste the back of beyond, but to penetrate the fastnesses so far beyond the back of beyond that any sense of normal sublunary existence is dissolved clean away. Only there can the mind be recalibrated and reinvented. Only there can a reality be confronted without the distortive overlay of anthropogenic dross. Here lies a kind of contradictory but creative misanthropy: only by shedding the trappings of mankind can a man's true nature be discerned. It is an ancient *modus operandi* in new clothes: reclusion as the road to enlightenment.

Yet it is so much more than that, for there is the sailing too. This withdrawal is a dynamic exercise, as physical as it is philosophical. It is a kind of automotive monasticism, somewhat more than filling a knapsack with bread and cheese and retiring to a distant cell. A yacht must be built, prepared and managed; long tracts of ocean must be navigated; every risk and eventuality must be assessed and provided for. Two interdependent journeys are to be made simultaneously, one of the body, one of the mind. The aim is to bring them both to the allotted point at the right pitch of readiness and receptiveness. Thus, in diverse ways, a long and solitudinous sea voyage is the *reductio ad absurdum* of the practice of pilgrimage.

The sailing and its demands are vital to the mix. The requisite harmonisation with wind and wave, the ceaseless concentration on every nuance of the physical environment, help free the mind and bring it into alignment with a world beyond itself. The physics and mechanics of it – a ton and a half of mass propelled so far, and with such grace, by no more than the movement of air and a few panels of simply-cut cloth – invite an aesthetic pleasure, along with a certain wonder and gratitude that energy and matter have arranged themselves thus. The endless rise and fall of the sea mimics the wave motions that underlie the fabric of the universe and the restlessness of all matter. Denied the false solidity of the terrestrial, one is more receptive to the truth that all is motion; that nothing is ever still, nor ever can be.

And there, perhaps, lies the conundrum: the goal is to find the key to an untrammelled peace –

a sphere rejoicing in its perfect stillness…

– but that stillness is, *a priori,* unattainable.

Nonetheless, the quest must continue; the voyage must be made, for every voyage brings its own reward, its own particular insight. To reject the voyage is to cede to a comforting urbanity; to accept the moribund and the uncritical. The time has not yet come for a living death.

Wester Ross
15th September 2017

INTRODUCTION

This is what I wanted to do: I wanted to sail my little yacht *Mingming II* into the heart of the Queen Victoria Sea. This sea lies to the north of Franz Josef Land. Franz Josef Land is an archipelago of 191 islands, or thereabouts, packed tightly in the Barents Sea well to the north of the Russian mainland. The islands belong to Russia, although the most westerly component of the group, Victoria Island, separated from the main group of islands by an eighty-mile-wide passage, was once Norwegian. The Norwegians ceded the island, which is much closer to the Svalbard group than Franz Josef Land, to the Russians during the 1930's, in a moment of political weakness. Victoria Island was first sighted in 1898 by the crew of the steam yacht *Victoria*, owned by the English adventurer Arnold Pike and skippered by a Captain Nielsen.

I discovered the existence of the Queen Victoria Sea on one of my Norwegian charts, while voyaging in the Barents Sea in 2014. There it was, sitting quietly to the north and west of the north-east looping Franz Josef Land islands: the *Victoriahavet*. I am a modest collector of seas, and so it immediately piqued my interest. I had never heard of it before; I doubt many sailors have. To sail into the Queen Victoria Sea would be difficult, but by no means impossible during a summer of minimal sea ice. As the sea has no clearly defined boundaries, I decided to take as its central point the position of the middle *i* in the *Victoriahavet* on my chart. This gave coordinates of 81° 36' North, 51° 12' East. That was my target. These days the edge of the Arctic pack-ice often recedes beyond 82°North towards the end of the summer. Most years it does, but sometimes it doesn't. As the centre of the Queen Victoria Sea is a distance of around 1700 nautical miles from my starting point in northern Scotland, and therefore about a month's sailing, it was impossible to know at outset whether there was any chance of success: in a month both sea ice and pack-ice can change their configuration considerably. In 2014 I sailed *Mingming II* to 79°North, to the east of Kong Karls Land. At that point I was starting to encounter small quantities of sea ice. However, 2014 was a summer in which the ice did not recede as much as it usually does nowadays. I was also relatively close to the calving glaciers of eastern Svalbard. Usually the sea further east is clearer of ice in mid-summer, giving a chance of a less troubled passage to the north-east and the western end of the main Franz Josef Land archipelago. Ultimately, all one can do is set sail and see for oneself.

That is the nuts and bolts of my original concept, from a purely navigational point of view: a voyage more or less due north from Scotland, passing to the east of Bear Island at 74° 30' North, heading north-north-east to cut between Victoria Island and the main Franz Josef Land group, before turning north-east into the Queen Victoria Sea itself; a voyage dictated, at its northern extremity, by the unpredictable vagaries of ice melt and movement; a nonstop voyage of about two months' duration, covering about 4000 nautical miles. Expressed in that way, it was a straightforward undertaking, but there is so much more to it. Why should I want to sail to such a barren tract of icy water? My target was no more than an arbitrary point on a hurtling sphere. There is nothing there to distinguish it from any other patch of Polar sea. As an expenditure of energy such a voyage is next to worthless. I am indifferent, moreover, to success or failure.

The simple fact is that now and again I like to go sailing. Or perhaps more accurately: from time to time I *need* to go sailing. By sailing I mean voyaging; keeping the sea for an extended period, and always, always, in the remotest of waters.

1

For nearly three years my mind had been elsewhere, but as the winter of early 2018 drew on I was drawn once more to my northern charts. I ordered books too, and as the gales cuffed the house night after night, I read my way deep into the exploration of Franz Josef Land and its surrounding seas. Here were tales of bravery and stupidity, unimaginable hardship, leadership exemplary, leadership disastrous and, mostly, failure followed by more failure. The Austrians came first, followed by the English and, in a series of ventures whose concept and execution swung between the comic and the tragic, the Americans. The Italians even put in an appearance. Tsarist Russia had no interest bar that of providing coal and dogs; the Norwegians provided ships and men for the high-spending Americans.

The aim of these expeditions, which spanned a forty-year period during the second half of the nineteenth and the early twentieth centuries, was to establish a base from which to make an attempt on the North Pole. The Pole was the great prize, and interest in Franz Josef Land was stimulated by the mistaken belief that somewhere up that way lay a great land mass, the mythic Zichy Land, that reached possibly to the Pole itself and could therefore serve as the bridge to fame and fortune. As time went on, that myth was discredited and dispelled, leaving nothing but a frozen, impenetrable sea. A number of lamentably inept attempts were made to cross that heaving mass of pressurized sea ice; not one of them got so far as to lose sight of Franz Josef Land just a few miles to the south before turning back. These were token sorties at best, designed to demonstrate to the expeditions' paymasters that the effort had at least been made.

Knowing in their hearts that the Pole was unreachable from Franz Josef Land, the explorers, ranging from the highly competent Frederick Jackson to the psychologically challenged Evelyn Briggs Baldwin, busied themselves with the exploration, mapping and naming of the archipelago itself. This was a grand displacement activity designed to appease the great and good of the time by naming every natural feature after them – islands, headlands, mountains, straits, bays and so on – in the hope thereby of alleviating the censure and disappointment the expedition leaders knew would be their lot once they returned home empty-handed.

The volumes I read over the winter were long and sometimes long-winded, but electrifying nonetheless. They brought my charts to life. I could now make sense of the puzzling Franz Josef Land nomenclature. I had long wondered why and how several hundred Russian islands and all their features were named for anyone and everyone except Russians. I could now read the stories behind each name: Nightingale Strait (Florence Nightingale, cousin of the English expedition leader Benjamin Leigh Smith); McClintock Island (Admiral Sir F. Leopold McClintock RN KCB FRS

LLD – provider of the Preface to Frederick Jackson's book *A Thousand Days in the Arctic*); Rudolph Island (named for Crown Prince Rudolph of Austria, son of the Emperor Franz Josef); Ziegler Island (named for the fabulously wealthy and infinitely gullible American baking powder tycoon William Ziegler, who financed both the Wellman and the Ziegler-Baldwin Polar Expeditions). Every name had its little aside.

These frigid islands came to life. Here was a whole history of mainly misguided human endeavour. The frozen headlands now pulsed with beating hearts; the snow and ice were red-raw with the trails of failed aspiration; my charts were now overlaid with a patina of suffering and intrigue. The brief summers here were treacherous, with snap storms and melting, oozing pack-ice; the winters were simply hellish. Every expedition had to overwinter, to be able to avail itself of the brief window in late spring when the weather had relented a little and daylight had returned, but the ice had not yet started to dissipate and could therefore be crossed in relative safety. During the dark months the men were confined to their tiny huts, living cheek by jowl in a stinking miasma of polar bear grease and walrus flesh and their own unsavoury smells.

My hours of reading finally yielded up what I was really looking for – the moment of the discovery and naming of the sea which was beckoning me on. I was pleased to find that the honour had fallen to Frederick G. Jackson, the Englishman of modest background, and probably the most disciplined and competent of the Franz Josef Land explorers. I quote here at some length from his almost-forgotten book, as these paragraphs provide an ideal vignette of both the appalling physical conditions the explorers had to put up with, and the unsentimental attitudes of the time. In this extract[1], Jackson is

---

1   From *A Thousand Days in the Arctic, Volume 1* by Frederick G. Jackson, Harper & Brothers 1899, pp.270-271

out on an exploratory foray along the north side of the islands, together with Albert B. Armitage, the eight-man expedition's scientist in charge of astronomical, meteorological and magnetic observations. Having found dogs to be of limited use on the difficult ice, Jackson advocated using ponies as well.

May 2ⁿᵈ, 1895, Thursday – Blowing a gale from the south-west, with heavy falling and driving snow, and the temperature has risen to 2° above freezing-point. All our furs and equipment are sopping wet, as is also the snow on the floes. I consulted with Armitage as to whether we had better proceed further, as we expect the ice south of us to break up and cut off our return, and we shall lose the ponies; and by risking it still further we can only follow this land a day or two farther along the coast, as an attempt to reach King Oscar Land – if such a land exists, which I much doubt – is quite out of the question now. Much of the ice we passed over further south was very thin and light – bay-ice, in fact. Armitage advocates an immediate return, and rightly so I think, as I don't feel justified in further risking our ponies for the sake of a day or two's further advance. Certainly nothing could look more threatening than the present state of things.

A she-bear and her cub, at least two years old, put in an appearance about 11a.m., and walked deliberately up to our camp. At forty yards I fired two shots successively aiming at her head, but to my surprise missed her with both. Still she and the cub stalked on quite unalarmed. I then discovered that in my haste, in pulling my 'militza' off over my head, I had humped up my muffler and chin-guard around my right cheek, giving me a false view along the sights, and causing my bad shooting. I put this matter right, and as she wheeled round, having become alarmed by the barking of the dogs, I shot her in the hind quarters, breaking her backbone low down, but she scrambled on, and as she slewed round at about seventy-five yards distance, I put a bullet through her heart and finished her. The cub, however, had cleared out, but hovered around in the distance for two hours, and then walked up to the body of his mother, when I gave him a shot through the head at about eighty yards. The she-bear was still suckling the cub, big as it was.

It is still blowing hard, snowing and driving, with thick mist, which partially lifted occasionally. We shall have to camp and wait till it is a little better. We had one of the kidneys, fried with bacon, of the bear I shot on the 30th inst. for breakfast. I took some of the meat for future use. Our latitude is 81° 19' 30" N., longitude 5° 18' 18" E., of Cape Flora (54° 55' 52" E.).

We had now reached a point a few miles to the northward of the spot where Nansen at the beginning of the following autumn arrived, and where he made his hut. We were fortunate in thus being the discoverers of this new country and of the sea to the north and north-west, which I named after our Queen – Queen Victoria Sea. The Cape where Nansen erected his hut some months later lay to the south-east of us.

Now that I had located the very moment and circumstance of the Sea's discovery, my resolve was strengthened. What had begun as an improbable idea almost four years earlier, as *Mingming II* and I plied our first passage through the Barents Sea, now became a kind of imperative. I had to sail where Jackson had seen nothing but ice, inhospitality, and impossibility. I had to know what it felt like to be at such an unlikely location on the planet; to see, too, whether I could unlock the navigational challenge of finding the best and most satisfying route into this almost unknown corner of the Arctic.

2

I had erected a sturdy shed to house *Mingming II* and so she waited, bone dry and in almost perfect condition, for our next adventure. I knew that the physical preparation for our next voyage would not take long, probably no more than a few weeks. The question as to when and if we would put to sea once more depended on one thing only – the state of the summer sea-ice. It was not only a matter of whether the ice would recede enough to allow passage into the Queen Victoria Sea, but also of this recession's configuration and timing. The edge of the pack-ice can move in an anarchic, constantly shifting way. Large patches of ice can become separated from the main body, they themselves roaming unpredictably according to wind and current. It would be easy to choose the wrong route; to reach an impasse when elsewhere free passage was available. If we were to succeed, I had to be sure of our trajectory, as the brief summer window was not long enough to allow for too much trial and error.

The actual timing of a voyage so far north had to be finely balanced. The ice continues to recede throughout most of the autumn, reaching its lowest coverage towards the end of October or thereabouts. To make a voyage so late in the year was, however, unthinkable. It would mean short days and cruel weather. A compromise had to be made between navigating in twenty-four hour daylight and relatively benign conditions, but with more ice around; and sailing later on in worse conditions but less ice.

My habit for previous Arctic voyages had been to leave Whitehills in northern Scotland towards the third or fourth week of June, with the aim of reaching my most northerly latitude towards the end of July and effecting a return passage by the end of August. I studied the ice movements for a number of previous years and concluded that for this voyage I would probably have to leave sometime around the third week in July – a month later than usual. This would mean a return passage in September. That was as late as I was prepared to contemplate.

My research showed that in 2016 and 2017 my proposed voyage would have been impossible. The ice had simply not receded adequately to the north of Franz Josef Land. This had been the case too in 2014, when we had turned back at 79° North, with the edge of the pack-ice just sixty miles further north.

I studied the ice and my charts and, as ever, tried to conceive of a shape to a voyage that would be both practical and satisfying. My two previous voyages, in *Mingming* and *Mingming II*, had included deviations out to the west to revisit Jan Mayen; the first voyage on the outward leg, the second on the return. I ruled this out as an option – it would add too much mileage to what may already be a long voyage with a strong easterly slant. My first thought was simply to sail to Kong Karls Land in the Barents Sea, as I had in 2014, before carrying on to the north-east in the hope of forcing a passage into the Queen Victoria Sea. This was practical enough, but the only viable return line was via a reciprocal course, making it a straight-out-and-back voyage. This had little appeal. I wanted if possible to find something with more shape to it.

It was at this point in my mental deliberations that a new and, at first, almost unthinkable possibility began to creep into the debate. It was this: what if we were to approach the Queen Victoria Sea not from the south, but from the west? What, therefore, if we were first to head due north, passing up the west side of the Svalbard group, before rounding the northern limit of those islands and heading east into our target waters? It was a concept that at first I dismissed as pie-in-the-sky. To go around the northern end of the island of Spitsbergen itself is a common enough venture, but to clear the whole group, lock stock and barrel, by passing to the north of the Sjuøyane – the Seven Islands – was a wholly different proposition. It would mean sailing to almost 81° North before turning fully east. Sometimes the Seven Islands remain locked in the ice for the whole summer; sometimes they clear a little. This voyage, if it were possible, would be somewhat longer. On the other hand, the shape of it – a clearly defined triangle into more or less un-sailed seas, the neatness of it, the near-outrageousness of it, all combined in a seductive mix that kept me coming back to the idea.

I decided to keep my options open. I now had two possible lines of approach; which one I took would depend on two things. The first and primary determinant would be state of the sea ice that year. By the time I sailed, if I felt that the ice was benign enough to allow passage, I ought to have a reasonable idea of what would or would not be possible. The second influence would be the weather once I had set sail. For example, if strong and persistent northerlies set in, a not unusual prospect, then I might be forced to cede by heading north-east into the Barents Sea. Storm force westerlies might have the same effect. Conversely, a run of strong easterlies would invite a passage up the west side of Svalbard.

The days lengthened and my winter's reading came to an end. My charts lay always to hand. I showed a few close friends what I had in mind. Tracing out the possible routes for them, while discussing the pros and cons of each, helped firm up my thinking and launched the process of converting the speculative to the real. To increase the pressure on myself and force that process along, I told family and friends that, ice permitting, this was the year I would sail.

By late spring I began to feel that I had regained the kind of commitment and motivation that is the absolute prerequisite for making a long and potentially challenging solo voyage. There is no room for half-heartedness in a venture of this kind; the mind must be tempered to a steely and indomitable sharpness. Little by little, every external distraction has to be pushed aside, bringing the central thought to a laser focus. Ultimately, there can be nothing but the voyage.

3

The days lengthened and the month of May arrived. I lowered *Mingming II* and her trailer off their blocks and towed her out of her shed into the fresh Highland air. This was the definitive statement of intent.

I made the usual lists and checked over all her gear, putting aboard the things which could endure a road journey, keeping the rest packed in large plastic containers. I replaced the battery for *Mingming II's* single electrical circuit, which feeds her solar-powered LED navigation lights, ran an extra bead of sealant around the edges of the hatch frames, overhauled her sail and made repairs and improvements to the batten end pockets. The mast had lain outside for three years, supported on trestles and tightly wrapped to protect it from wind and rain. I unwrapped it and checked over the running rigging.

The lower bearing of my Windpilot Pacific Light self-steering gear, a cylindrical Tufnol bearing inside an aluminium alloy tube, had seized solid. This had happened before, as it is difficult to wash out any residual salt water. In the past I had been able to free it up with liberal applications of penetrating oil and gentle manual pressure. This time nothing would budge. I did not dare apply too much pressure in case I broke something. Finally I contacted Peter Förthman, who manufactures the Windpilot, to see what he would suggest I do. The answer came back quickly: try a silicon-based lubricating oil, as this has the ability to break down the salt crystals which were no doubt jamming the bearing. It worked. For several days I kept on applying the oil and manipulating the whole gear until it was once again almost friction-free. It is difficult to overstate the importance of a strong and efficient self-steering unit for a solo sailor. My Windpilot had thus far steered me across 24,000 miles of ocean, and was by far the best and most trusted member of my generally shifty crew.

I drove over to the east coast to buy all my non-perishable victuals. The basics for my main meal of the day were packed as usual into big yellow flare containers, each one labelled to show how many meals it contained. This gave me about seventy meals which, with the addition of extra food stored in lockers, combined with a more rigorous regime, would enable to keep the sea for up to a hundred days. Rough calculations had suggested that the proposed voyage might take about sixty-eight days, so I had plenty of spare capacity should we be slowed down or incapacitated in some way. I baked seventy-five flapjacks, well-loaded with nuts and dried fruit, and packed them away in watertight containers. Using ingredients bought wholesale I made up about five kilograms of trail mix, this too stored in watertight containers. I checked over my water cans and bottles, leaving the final filling until I got to Whitehills. This would save transporting the weight of the seventy litres I carry, and ensure that throughout the voyage I drank nothing but sweet Moray water, the same as used for the distilling of some of Scotland's finest whiskies.

Every day I checked the condition of the Arctic sea ice, and as June progressed I began to notice that something unusual was happening. Since the end of April, the ice in the northern Barents Sea has receded from about 76° North to almost 82° North. I could not remember having seen anything like it. Over a period of about eight weeks the east-west line of the ice edge had moved north approximately three hundred and sixty nautical miles – an average of forty-five miles per week. Here was a phenomenal rate of ice melt and movement. Already, the northern extremity of the Svalbard group seemed to be well clear of ice, as was all but the most northerly fringe of the Queen Victoria Sea. Ice still clung to the northern islands of Franz Josef Land, centring on Rudolph Island, the most northerly member of the group.

Seeing this, and taking the view that by the time I reached that far, if I were able, the ice would have moved further north, I began to think about another target to aim for. Most of the explorers who had made attempts on the North Pole from Franz Josef Land had used as their jumping off point the area around Cape Fligely on Rudolph Island. This is the most northerly headland, not just of Franz Josef Land, but of the whole of Eurasia. It lies just above 81° 50' North. I began to introduce Cape Fligely into the mental picture of the voyage. As ever, it was neither a hard and fast target, nor any kind of imperative; simply a fascinating possibility, and one that might give a firmer sense of direction to my peregrinations, should I be fortunate enough to get as far as the Queen Victoria Sea.

The rapidity of the ice movement had caught me by surprise and forced a hasty reconsideration of the timing of the voyage. There was now nothing to be gained by waiting until the latter half of July before setting sail. It was as well that I had started my preparations well in advance, as I was able to bring forward my proposed start time by three or four weeks without any problem. I was intensely happy at being able to do this. I would get the best of the long days in the Arctic, and, all being well, would make the return voyage before the nastier autumnal weather set in. As long as I was not delayed waiting for a suitable weather window for starting out, I would be leaving only a week or so later than my previous High Arctic voyages. This reintroduced a comforting ambiance of ease and familiarity into the project.

What had begun as something of an improbable, or even an impossible, notion, had now become a definite possibility. It was a matter of pure luck that in the year I was ready to sail again, the ice had been so cooperative. There was no guarantee that these exceptional conditions would repeat themselves in subsequent years. This combination of my desire to sail and the evolution of the most appropriate ice conditions imaginable gave a sense of rightness to the voyage and strengthened my confidence and resolve. My focus narrowed. As each day passed I sloughed off layer after layer of dull, terrestrial distraction, moving my mind surely seawards towards the rhythm of the wave and the pure line of an ever-shifting horizon.

4

On the last Monday of June I got up at two in the morning and with *Mingming II* hitched astern of my pick-up, drove from the west coast of the Highlands due east to our 'home' port of Whitehills on the Moray Firth. This took a mere three and a half hours – not much more than a school run compared to our previous fifteen-hour nonstop hauls from Burnham-on-Crouch on the Essex coast.

Once arrived, I set to preparing *Mingming II* for launch. A mobile crane had been ordered for later in the day from nearby Macduff shipyard by my invaluable friend and local farmer Jimmy Forbes. Whitehills is still as much a working fishing port, though with its activity much reduced compared to former times, as a leisure marina, so even at six in the morning there was a fair bustle of preparation and unloading of lobster boats. As I worked, a constant stream of old friends came to say hello. The harbourmaster, Bertie Milne, was soon there too, and we quickly finalised the exact point where

Mingming II would be put into the water, and the berth she would be towed to by a rope line set across the harbour.

This was the fourth Arctic voyage I had made from Whitehills, so our routines were well established. By early afternoon *Mingming II* was afloat, with her mast stepped, and snug in the berth she would keep until we set sail. I began the long job of moving the sail, all of a piece with its yard, boom and battens, from its road travelling position along the starboard side-deck, to its fully rigged sea-going state. This involved setting up the main halyard as a hoist to lift the heavy sail bundle high enough to slide the forward end between the mast and the lift – the line from the masthead, looped with a bowline around the base of the mast, which holds the boom and sail bundle in position. Then the three loops of the lazyjacks cum topping lifts were worked from aft under the boom and secured in their stainless steel eyes. With the sail bundle now properly supported fore and aft I could work away slowly and methodically lashing the individual batten parrels in place and setting up the sail's control lines: main halyard, six-part mainsheet, yard-hauling parrel and luff-hauling parrel.

The complexity of the junk rig lies in its set-up rather than its management once at sea. It is a supremely intelligent system which spreads all the loads on mast and sail as evenly as possible, avoiding stress-points and thereby minimising structural failures. Once the relatively complex array of ropework has been correctly set up, the sail becomes a soft and infinitely variable motive force, controlled easily from a single position.

As I laboured away I had the usual string of visitors, curious to see how it all worked. I gave my standard reefing demonstration, showing how the full twenty-eight square metre sail could be reduced to any size, even just a couple of square feet, within a few seconds using only one hand. I had no illusions that I would convert any of my Bermudan sailor visitors, as impressed as they were. I have long since accepted that the occidental mind is too wedded to the shiny, the technologically complex and the heavily marketed to be persuaded by glaringly obvious but roughly constructed mechanical efficiency and simplicity.

I slept on board for the first time in nearly four years, enjoying the soft surge of a sea calmed almost to smoothness by its passage through the outer harbour. *Mingming II* strained gently against her mooring lines. I lay on my back, eyes closed, and drew my thoughts back in, honing them to razor sharpness, feeling the boat in its entirety, merging myself back into its beauty and its possibility.

The next day I worked again on the rig, hoisting the sail time after time, adjusting and readjusting until I was satisfied that I had everything set up as well as possible. Once there was no more I could do I wrapped the sail bundle tightly in its cover and began the task of bringing all my stores on board and stowing everything in its allotted place. I pulled out all the water containers onto the pontoon, rinsed them thoroughly and filled them with whisky water. *Mingming II* settled a little further on her marks as the water came back on board. The cabin moved slowly from chaos to order and began to adopt its proper sea-going persona.

To complete the day I walked up to the pub for a pint and a plate of fish and chips.

After a little more tidying up the next morning, I set off for home. Jimmy Forbes had already taken *Mingming II*'s trailer up to his farm for safe-keeping during the voyage.

All that remained now was to organise my house and croft for the two months or so that I was likely to be away. This was made easy by the kindness of friends and neighbours in the remote little enclave that is now home. They assumed their appropriate responsibilities, organised casual rotas to ensure everything was kept an eye on, and thus made it possible for me to abandon the land and buildings into which I had already invested so much of my time and labour.

I made my final study of the ice maps. The northern extremity of Svalbard was well clear; Rudolph Island and the other northern islands of Franz Josef Land were still locked in the edge of the pack-ice, but only just. The unknown factor was loose sea ice, which does not always register on the satellite-generated maps, but which can be just as dangerous, if not more so, than solid pack-ice. I had no idea whether I was likely to meet any random concentrations, or isolated floes, or whether I would have clear passage. There was only one way to find out.

My other growing focus was the short-term weather prognosis. My general rule is to set sail with the prospect of at least two, and preferably three, days of a fair wind, in order to get clear of land, fishing boats, oil rigs and commercial shipping lanes as quickly as possible. The outlook was mixed, with predominantly high pressure forecast and a good chance of cyclonic conditions.

I set off for Whitehills once more on the morning of Monday 2nd July, stopping at a supermarket on the way to buy my last-minute fresh stores: sixty green apples, a large hand of green bananas, a couple of long-life loaves, five kilograms or so of various hard and long-lasting cheeses – Cheddar, Cheshire, Jarlsberg, Gouda, Emmental, Gruyère and the like. The check-out girl commented on the quantity and range of the cheese. She was a cheese-lover too. I resisted telling her that it was all bound for the High Arctic and an unknown sea.

5

Arriving at Whitehills, I had not known whether I would be setting sail within a day or two, or whether I would have to wait a week or even longer. I stowed my final stores and watched the fluttering of the flags around the harbour and the masthead wind indicators of the moored yachts. A faint north-easterly was blowing – the worst of winds. I remembered being confined to harbour for the best part of ten days with constant north-easterlies.

Nonetheless, I had to be ready. I drove my pick-up to Jimmy's farm to join *Mingming II's* trailer for the duration of the voyage, and came back with him in his Land Rover. I stood talking with Jimmy on the harbour wall and noticed that the wind was starting to veer a little. It was hauling round to the east. I was now scarcely listening to what Jimmy was saying. The breeze on my cheek was distracting me, calling me out to sea. Perhaps it was time to go, right now, this very minute.

I said my goodbyes and thankyou to Jimmy and went into Bertie Milne's office. He brought up a wind forecast on his computer. Winds would be light, but it looked like there might be a couple of days of east or south-east winds. With so much high pressure around I did not want to waste them.

'I think I've got to be off, Bertie.'

'Nae bother. Would you like to make an executive decision and give me a precise time?' Bertie has a dry sense of humour and would as usual be towing us out to sea in his son-in-law's open boat *Swee'Pea*.

'Fifteen minutes?'

'Nae bother.'

It was pretty much a carbon copy of our previous departure from Whitehills. At two fifteen on the afternoon of Monday 2nd July, I passed our tow rope to local berth-holder Graeme Gordon, who was helping Bertie aboard *Swee'Pea*, and slipped our mooring lines. We made our way through to the outer harbour, turned hard to starboard into the entrance channel, and rode the light swell out to the broad waters of the Moray Firth.

The wind was still in the east, with perhaps a hint of north in it too, but it was a steady Force 3 under a brilliant blue sky. I hauled up six panels of the sail and pulled our tow rope back on board. With *Mingming II* sailing full and bye, and prancing forward with an instant and refreshing purpose, I hooked up the self-steering gear and settled her to her course. *Swee'Pea* circled us for a while and Bertie took photographs. We surged on as distance from the land freshened the breeze. *Mingming II* heeled gently to the pressure of the wind, her bow cutting white streaks into the swell. *Swee'Pea* turned for home and was soon no more than a turquoise dot astern.

We were on our own and the voyage, so long considered, was now reality. I had often wondered whether I would find again that wellspring of intent, but here we were once more, retracing our well-worn track along North 30° East magnetic. Ahead lay fifteen hundred miles or so of sailing to bring us to the north-west coast of Spitsbergen, should I feel minded to take that route, and should the winds allow. I relished the idea of this long haul, its meatiness and its lack of compromise. If I were to round the top of Svalbard then there could be no distraction from the task of making northing, day after day, week after week.

At four thirty a red ship with a white superstructure passed a mile or so ahead of us, heading west. The line of Moray and Aberdeenshire hills thinned to a narrow and undulating streak on the southern horizon. The wind veered a little towards the east, freeing us to a shy reach, and *Mingming II* slid quietly and smoothly on. The horizon ahead sharpened to a Euclidian precision under a sky unblemished by the slightest cloud. I sat in the hatchway, revelling once more in the spring and movement of my little ship and the prospect of the adventure to come.

6

It was not, ultimately, the fast and free-flowing departure I had half expected, for the wind drifted slowly off to caress other sailors in other seas. By one in the morning we were becalmed. By three we were under way again under seven panels. By six thirty we were once more heaving to the swell with the sail bundle well-lashed to the boom gallows. It was that kind of weather – little winds coming in from anywhere for an hour or two before sneaking off to leave us once more idle.

I really did not care. A harbour porpoise rolled softly by and a noisy and rather old-style blue and white fishing boat headed south. As we worked our way past the west side of the Captain Oil Field, a big orange RIB from one of the rigs headed straight for us, throwing up an extravagant and noisy V of a bow wave, circled a few times, her crew pointing and taking photographs, then sped off back to base. We were evidently some sort of curiosity to be examined, nothing more. They could have throttled back their horsepower, lain quietly alongside for a minute or two, passed the time of day, *had a gam* as I think the old-timers used to say, been just a little personable, but instead – nothing but pointing, snapshots, and gone.

The wind took itself to the north-west and a great skua headed purposefully west on skua business. The wind faded and we idled once more under a hot sun. We had nonetheless covered fifty miles in the twenty-two hours since leaving Whitehills; the Arctic was fifty miles closer. A faint zephyr came up from the east and we started to tangle with fishing boats working the north end of the Little Halibut Bank. A kittiwake tried to land on the masthead. The wind held in the east and a strange-looking ship, a kind of gigantic landing craft, passed ahead, bound south-east. I switched on the navigation lights.

It was all so familiar and so comforting, this never-ending procession: objects animate and inanimate criss-crossing in their fall through space. I was already so firmly back at sea that I might never have been away. The timing and the fine detail might differ, but the generality is always the same: ships, birds, whales, winds; briefly intersecting trajectories; random recognitions; chaos and instability.

On Wednesday morning a gutless west-south-westerly metamorphosed to an imperceptible north-easterly, bringing mist with it. A kittiwake took up residence on the foredeck, rent-free. A ship's foghorn gave two blasts. The wind veered to the east, freeing us once more, and weak sunshine pierced the fog. We bubbled softly past a razorbill and her chick. The sky grew more overcast, more promising of wind.

At nine fifteen that morning the entire City of Scunthorpe appeared out of the gloom to our west, re-packaged as a towering cruise ship. It filled the western quadrant end to end and stretched skywards, deck after sandwiched deck of it, up and up, an outrageous displacement of sea and air, and somehow moving itself along with the quiet determination of a giant, unworldly slug. The whole city was packed in there, for sure, all eighty-two thousand souls, or thereabouts, along with the accoutrements and necessities of gracious onboard living: swimming pools and dance floors, massage parlours and bowling alleys, bars and banks, theatres, shops, gymnasia, perhaps a university or two, municipal parks, churches, mosques, synagogues, a morgue for the expiring, a delivery room for the arriving, promenades for walking and chat rooms for talking; a floating, automotive metropolis. I wondered whether such a contraption marked the apotheosis of misconceived pleasure-seeking. Was there a kind of insane rationale here: citizens escaping the perceived drabness of the city by a provisional flight into a purely escapist replica? I watched the thing slide smoothly by and overwhelmed my mind with calculations as to the plumbing requirements for the washing, showering, teeth-brushing and toilet-flushing of the eighty-two thousand needy organisms on board.

Scunthorpe re-packaged disappeared into the mist astern and the wind eased. An hour later, even though we were well upwind, I could still catch a whiff or two of the greasy cooking smells pumped from the city's kitchen ventilators: the rancid, spent odour of indulgence now spread across the surface of the monster's track; the olfactory spoor of advanced civilisation.

Later that day we crossed 59° North and I awarded myself a Fox's Glacier Mint. Our stop-start progress continued in the intermittent patches of moving air. A faint zephyr from the south proved un-sailable – our forward movement cancelled out the apparent wind from astern, rendering the wind vane ineffective. I invented a counter-intuitive strategy to get around the problem: by reducing the sail to just three panels and by thus rebalancing the relationship between our forward movement and the apparent wind, the Windpilot was no longer confused and so rediscovered its purpose.

We ghosted gently on through the not-quite-night of those latitudes. I dozed on and off in my bunk until a suspicious vibration invaded the ambient sounds of a smoothly running yacht, bringing me to the hatch and the sight of a Spanish fishing boat, trawl set, bearing down on us. A rapid disengagement of the self-steering and a hardening up to a shy reach diffused the danger of imminent collision.

Within an hour or two we finally found release from the weak cyclonic gyrations which had kept our progress muted. The wind went round to the south-west and found some vigour. I gybed to head due north and *Mingming II* skipped forward with a will. By eight in the morning the sky had cleared, the wind had veered to a fresh west-north-westerly and there we were at last, plunging Arctic-wards in an indigo, white-tossed sea, a fine, uncompromising sailor's sea under a fine, uncompromising sailor's wind. All doubt was dispelled as to whether I had skipped port prematurely. By midday Sumburgh Head, Shetland's southerly point, was square on the port beam. We had covered almost a hundred and fifty miles since leaving Whitehills, and were now well set to take advantage of the westerly change.

7

From time to time vessels still passed, each one observed intensely during the minute or two of its proximity, each one demanding its backstory. Here was another blue and white fishing boat, LK 23, and so a local fellow, trawling to windward on our port quarter. Who was the skipper? Murdo Macrae? John Moriston? Did he have a wife back home in Lerwick? How long had he been at the fishing? Did he drive a BMW or an Audi, like most hard-done-by fishermen? Had he been involved in the great Shetland fishery scandal[2]? The questions piled on until LK 23 was hull down and out of mind forever.

Later a super-sleek yacht, at least seventy feet overall, Dutch-flagged, crossed astern heading west, motor-sailing to windward under a reefed mainsail. She seemed to be doing a good seven or eight knots, flinging her bow skywards

---

2 A mechanism had been installed at Lerwick to divert part of the catch away from quota inspectors.

as she breasted each wave, a triumph of technology over nature. Once more the questions came flooding in. What was the hurry that demanded such a crude and uncomfortable mode of progress? Was a table already booked at a Lerwick restaurant? Was the prospect of a night at sea too much to bear? How had Jan or Koos or Hendrik made his money? How many crew were aboard (I could only see a single helmsman)? Was this their first passage to Shetland? Had they noticed the deep-reefed junk sail to their north?

Overnight I hand-steered for a while to work around another fishing vessel. After breakfast I had an almost complete change of clothes, donning a more sea-going rig of loose, comfortable clothing. A helicopter flew overhead, bound north-east, clearing our masthead by several thousand feet. The sun came out and the familiar whaleback of Unst, seen so many times on so many voyages, inscribed its curve low above the western horizon.

At local noon, just for the hell of it, I took a meridian altitude with my trusty Ebbco sextant. Like its owner, it was getting old and battered and error-prone. With such a low height of eye on a pitching, rolling boat, and with the sun kissing the horizon directly behind the wind vane, and with an uncertain index error, it was a struggle to get a reliable sight. I ended up sixteen minutes of latitude, or sixteen nautical miles, north of my true latitude. I knew well enough that I would soon improve with practice, and resolved to keep at it. This turned out to be a vain resolution, as the sun and all the celestial bodies were to remain hidden for most of the voyage.

That afternoon I made my first exit of the hatch to check over the self-steering gear, impelled aft by an occasional and unnerving graunching sound. I could find nothing wrong. Perhaps it was one of the steering line blocks. I lubricated everything as well as I could and returned below to cook the first standard sea-going meal of the voyage. For the first four days I had been eating quick and improvised meals knocked up from my fresh stores: sandwiches made with fresh bread, plenty of butter and filled with cheese, tomato, tinned tuna in various sauces, along with bananas and homemade flapjacks. This allowed me to prepare and eat my food quickly, freeing me up to concentrate on watchkeeping and navigation as we made our way through the more crowded coastal waters. It also eked out my stores by a few more days, thereby giving me a longer potential sea-keeping capacity, should it be needed. I now began the switch to my proper regime, cooking a pan of hot food in the evening, a third of which would be kept and reheated for breakfast.

We were now to the north-east of the Shetlands and the sea began to change character as the longer pelagic swells curled in from the west. I started to breathe more easily with the land now gone. There were still oil rigs to our north-east, but the dangers and obstacles were falling away.

It was about this time that my intention to sail directly to the north-west coast of Spitsbergen began to firm up. What had been a loose idea now became an all-consuming objective. I realised that I had needed a few days at sea in order to build a foundation for my resolve. I had needed to feel *Mingming II* surging forward beneath me; to feel myself once more relaxed and at ease with the incessant daily round of singlehanded ship management; to feel myself once more subsumed into this oceanic world, at once alien and familiar, seductive and repellent, intoxicating and sobering. The possible diversions – Jan Mayen to the west, Bear Island to the east – would be left to the return leg, if at all. I began to think too of the satisfaction I might derive if I could take us through the same spot at 80°North that I had reached in *Mingming* in 2011, thereby continuing the trajectory of that voyage, pushing the same line further on. I thought once more about the Spitsbergen coast, with its landscape of close-packed toothy peaks overseeing an ocean bristling with the tall spouts of fin whales, and felt a sudden and untypical longing to be back there. For the first time I felt that both heart and mind were fused in their intent, that I was now operating with an indivisible unity of purpose. It was a heady, wholesome feeling. I was back to doing what I had to do. There was no especial logic it to it, no purpose other than the act itself. I was impelled by nothing more than my nature, but a man at one with his nature is a rare and happy organism.

I settled in the hatch and watched the gaps in the cloud to the north. They burned a deep and fiery red.

8

We had already had to alter course several times to avoid almost certain collisions with other ships upon the sea. I had many times puzzled over the statistical unlikelihood of this. There we were, a little yacht just a few feet in beam, heading north through what was now a wide and almost empty ocean, and yet our trajectory seemed drawn to those of the one or two craft that were still about. As will be seen, this came to be one of the recurring themes of the voyage: our uncanny ability to chance directly and precisely upon any sea-borne hazard.

The following morning, as we approached 62°North, the latitude which defined the northern limit of any permanent hazards, it happened again. We were heading, with unerring accuracy, straight for a small and very modern-looking ship that appeared to be holding a stationary position. I altered course fifteen degrees to the east to keep well clear of it. The ship seemed to be guarding two sets of buoys set a hundred metres or so apart. Seeing our approach, it moved into position directly behind the buoys, perhaps to make sure we kept clear of them. It was an extraordinarily plush-looking craft, with a high-sided blue hull and a sparkling white superstructure that exuded modernity and sleek design. The high central bridge was glazed with an unbroken sweep of dark glass that added to the general impression of sophistication. What was it doing here? Maybe it was some sort of scientific survey ship. As we passed I was able to make out its name: the *Leinebris* of Fosnavaag.

Subsequent research showed that we had chanced upon the most modern longliner of the Norwegian fishing fleet, fifty-eight metres and two and a half thousand tons of technological wizardry designed to extract, gut, fillet, pack and freeze its harvest with maximum efficiency and in one smooth operation. The automated lines are set from inside the ship, via a so-called 'moonpool', a more or less vertical shaft through the ship's innards, which allows the crew to work in total protection from the elements. This was the fisherman's version of the *City of Scunthorpe*, with its gymnasium, sauna, solarium, sky lounge with a 60-inch television and so on. I thought of the hard-drinking, hard-fighting trawlermen I had encountered during a Sixties' summer spent bingo-calling on Rose's Pier in Lowestoft, and wondered what they would make of it all.

We left the *Leinebris* astern and I contemplated the long arms of cirrus fanning out from the north-western sky. They had an ugly look about them and I wondered whether *Mingming II* may be about to experience her first really heavy weather. The wind backed to the south-west, and our noon position showed a daily run of eighty-five nautical miles. We were getting along famously.

With freshening conditions on the port quarter we ran north, straight as a die, now fully liberated from any navigational constraints, free to roam wherever winds and whimsy took us, firmly settled to the rhythm of the voyage proper. The sun graced us for an hour or two and a ship passed several miles astern, heading west. Patches of murk came and went, as unpredictably as the now veering, now backing wind. Yes, the wind was forever shifting this way and that, but within a narrow vector, and always centred on the west or thereabouts, and so it was a fair wind, always blowing at an honest strength, that would give us a hundred miles of northing noon to noon.

Later the next morning an excitement of fulmars and great skuas, the kind of screaming, chaotic frenzy that accompanies the passage of cetaceans, yielded two quick glimpses of the fins of female killer whales. Behind them, on the western horizon, a great mass of cloud, supported by columns of thick rain, put me in mind of Brighton Pier.

The wind wound itself up a little harder and I reduced sail to just half a panel, enough to keep us plunging comfortably on at a couple of knots or so. There was nothing threatening in the blow, but I took one or two simple precautions, from habit as much as anything else, and to maintain the sense of control and discipline that keeps the mind always relaxed and untroubled: I lashed the long pendants fixed to the top batten around the boom gallows, ensuring that the sail bundle would always firmly remain in place; and dogged down all the hatches and the aft portlight, effectively sealing the boat. With such a snug and well-protected configuration, the heavier weather outside was defused to no more than an inconvenience, everything was dry and quiet below, and *Mingming II* felt reassuringly indomitable.

It was short-lived, this half gale, and of little consequence, but it served to bring us fully back to the rhythms of a long passage, with its incessant adjustments and re-adjustments; its proliferation of small detail; its ultimate harmonisation of skipper and craft. The wind soon came off, and by the next morning we were back to our full working rig of six panels, the sea being still too confused to risk the final panel and the wringing it might encourage at the masthead.

Our first week at sea was up and I reviewed the statistics. Noon to noon straight line positions had totalled nearly six hundred and thirty nautical miles – an average of seventy miles a day. I had altered the amount of sail we were carrying almost fifty times – about once every four hours on average. I had exited the hatch just once. With our latitude now at about 64° 45'North, we were less than a hundred and ten miles from the Arctic Circle.

It was as good a start to the voyage as I could reasonably have expected. We were well into the Norwegian Sea with the winds set fair, and on the very threshold of the Arctic. I had already gone a long way towards the full casting off of the land-bound persona, sloughing off and leaving well astern, layer by layer, the cloying, restrictive wrappings of social conformity. Confined to my tiny cell on a wide ocean, I could now seek liberation. Under a cloudless sky I sat in the hatchway and watched the rippling line of the horizon. The hiss-hiss-hiss of the waves on the quarter lulled me to a semi-trance. The world became timeless; I became ageless. For a little while there was nothing but the pulse of the universe and the enchantment of its unceasing motion.

9

As we crossed into the Arctic, I reflected that I had done so twice in *Mingming,* a 20' 6" Corribee, and now twice in *Mingming II*, a 23'9" Achilles 24. I felt sure that a significant statistic lurked somewhere behind these figures. After a great deal of pencil-sucking, I calculated firstly that I had sailed north into the Arctic four times in yachts averaging 21'10½" in length. That gave an uncorrected Arctic Index of 5'5⅝" per northerly crossing. The Arctic Index – average length of craft divided by number of crossings – was of course a spontaneous invention of my own and one which, like all reductions of human activity to no more than its fundamental numerical basis, gave a curiously pleasing and somehow insightful re-statement of that activity.

The uncorrected Arctic Index, as it stood, was a somewhat crude measure, clearly in need of refinement. It needed firstly the application of an Age Factor. This I determined should be 100 ÷ average age at crossings. In my case that gave 100

÷ 66.25 = 1.5. My Age-adjusted Arctic Index was therefore 5'5⅝" x 1.5 = 8' 2 ⁷⁄₁₆". I felt now that I was starting to get to the mathematical heart of the matter. All that needed to be allowed for now was the Crew Factor. That was a simple and final adjustment – the multiplication of the Age-adjusted Arctic Index by the average number of crew on board over all the crossings. For a consistently singlehanded sailor the Age-related Arctic Index is simply multiplied by one, therefore remaining unchanged.

The net result of this byzantine analysis was to give me a Personal Arctic Indicator (PAI) of 8' 2 ⁷⁄₁₆". The lower the figure the better, as it reduces with the number of crossings, age and smallness of craft. Having arrived at this numerical reduction of my Arctic incursions, I felt inordinately puffed up. The 7/16ths, in particular, gave the final result an air of unassailable accuracy. The number swirled around in my head – eight feet two inches and *seven sixteenths*. Everyone knows (I kidded myself) that to achieve a PAI of eight feet three inches is pretty good, but I had pipped it by an additional *nine sixteenths*. I fell instantly in love with those *nine sixteenths* and resolved never, ever, to take them for granted.

One vexatious point remained. Was I really sailing singlehanded? Could the shadowy figures who skulked around in the darker corners of *Mingming II* be considered additional crew or not? As it happened, the usual ship's complement had been increased by a new appointment solely for this voyage, following the replacement of fruit cake in the ship's stores by trail mix. The issuing of handfuls of nuts and dried fruit several times a day is a skilled job, and so an (allegedly) trained Ship's Distributor of Nuts had been signed up. The full ship's complement was now:

Captain
Doctor *and* Dentist
Collector of Rain
Distributor of Nuts
Cabin Boy

The latest addition to the Ship's manifest, the Distributor of Nuts, doled out his niggardly rations two or three times a day, before slinking off back to his lair under the cockpit. He had long and hygienically suspect fingers which plunged deeply into the container of mixed nuts, seeds and dried fruit, arousing expectations of an imminent orgy of munching. As his digits rose in the air, however, everything they held, bar a few wizened cashews and a currant or two, trickled back down whence it had come. I was reminded of one of those remotely operated grabs found in seaside amusement arcades, which have no difficulty picking up fluffy toys or imitation Rolex watches, but which without fail manage to drop them before reaching the exit chute.

He was an implacable bastard, unmoved by any form of appeal, even for so little as one extra sunflower seed.

Once, just once, I was moved to say something:

But…but I need more! I'm the Captain!

Captain? Ha! Couldn't captain a rowin' boat on the Serpentine, you couldn't. Don't you 'Captain' me, matey. Funniest thing I heard in a long while that is. Captain, my arse! You'll get what you're given, sunshine. Take it or leave it.

By virtue of his taciturnity and his contempt for anyone unversed in his own particular skill, he slotted perfectly into the existing band of misfits that peopled *Mingming II* from stem to stern. All in all, they were a pretty unwholesome bunch, encompassing the pompous and the prissy, the slovenly and the indolent, every man Jack of them shot through with the wordless insolence of the subordinate who knows best. They were, though, an evanescent little band, somehow insubstantial, chimerical, easily secreted beneath the cabin sole, and so not any kind of real threat to my status as a lone sailor.

10

During my previous Arctic voyages, I had learned that to reach that state of grace which can reign in the High Arctic in midsummer – a perpetual and obliquely-orbiting sun turning placid seas to deep indigo and transforming ice to gargantuan diamonds – one must first endure the rite of passage in which the sun's very existence comes into doubt. Between roughly 66°North and 76°north, a distance of some six hundred nautical miles, one must run the gauntlet of sunless day after sunless day, of choking overcast and fog, of heavy, featureless cloud, and of a creeping, insistent cold and damp. One could easily be forgiven for losing faith. After ten or twelve days of oppressive gloom, the prospect of an eventual emergence into the radiant North grows less and less credible. Even the initiated can start to doubt that beyond this seemingly never-ending pall there will be a brilliance and sparkle of a quality found in few places on this planet. The lurking thought is always the same: perhaps this time things will be different and all I will get for my trouble is nothing but a voyage cloaked interminably in cold and fog.

On Wednesday 11th July, ten days out from Whitehills, I found a hazy sun for long enough to take another meridian altitude, this time with less than two miles of error. The pleasure I derived from this may well have been moderated, had I known that henceforward the sun itself would play little part in our voyage. This was a year in which the prevailing meteorological conditions were all skewiff. The Jetstream had moved considerably further north than usual, allowing high pressure and heatwaves to dominate in Europe but, as I was to discover, squeezing the Arctic High further north and somehow robbing it of its usual sparkle.

With a predominantly south-westerly wind on the port quarter we were clocking up daily runs of between eighty and ninety-five miles, and so I laboured under the illusion that before too long we would leave the gloom behind.

My eating regime had by then found its settled form for this voyage:

6 a.m.	Breakfast	The leftovers from the previous night's dinner.
8 a.m.		Piece of chocolate.
10 a.m.		Two handfuls of trail mix.
12 a.m.	Lunch	Rye bread, butter, cheese, marmite or jam. Flapjack. Apple.
6 p.m.	Dinner	Rice or pasta or potato with tinned vegetables and tinned fish. Custard, rice pudding or bottled fruit. Two handfuls of trail mix.
Night-time		Energy bar if necessary.

It was a simple and nutritious diet, well-honed over many years of sailing, that kept me lean and healthy throughout a voyage. It was quick and easy to prepare too, and used only a minimal amount of cooking fuel.

The wind veered to the west and a young Pomarine skua investigated us for a minute or two. Fog came in, and with it the first northern phase fulmar of the voyage – a dull mucky-pup of a bird compared to his gleaming white southern cousins.

We reached 71°North, with Jan Mayen a hundred and eighty miles to our west and the North Cape of Norway to our east. The continent of Europe was falling away astern. Ahead lay nothing but islands and ice. The fog thickened. We seemed to pass through a patch of colder water, signalled by a sudden drop in temperature inside the cabin. I spent an hour or so in the forehatch, shortening and re-lashing the batten parrels, the lines which hold the sail battens to the mast. The fog cleared almost to the horizon, then swirled back in again. The wind backed to the east-south-east and so I gybed to a broad reach, bringing us somewhat east of north and on course for Prins Karls Forland.

I wondered again about this imperative to keep sailing north. Every degree of northing brought its own surge of pleasure. Our insistent northerly track was both a movement away and a movement towards; an even balance of repulsion and attraction. As the seas around grew more alien and empty, I felt more solid, more substantial. It had always been thus. Even as a child, roaming the deep woods that stretched for miles from our North Wales' cottage, I had always been drawn on to the furthest and most hidden corners. In finding where the nuthatches nested and the whitethroats sang, in learning the patterns of the pools where the brown trout lurked, in seeking out the deepest silence of the forest, I found also a path to my own core. Here now was the same principle, the same fundamental need, transferred to a bigger scale. Sixty years on, was I still a child at heart, or had my juvenile wanderings been a presentiment of adulthood? Did it matter anyway? The compulsion to seek out the wild places was so deep-seated and constant that it bore no relationship to maturity or immaturity; it was as much a part of me as the nose on my face. I suspected that this was why I had always felt such ease at sea. I was not in any way forcing myself into something that felt unnatural or intimidating. To be alone and well off the beaten track was a state I had cultivated since early childhood. The pelagic environment was in many ways alien, for sure, but it was alienation of a kind which I had always sought. It did not unnerve me in any way. I welcomed it, rather than feared it.

I thought about this and wondered too whether these later-life voyages to the very heart of remoteness were a subconscious attempt to resurrect the unmediated feelings of my youth. Was I trying to rediscover or recreate something which I had lost forever – the ability to see the world through the eyes of a ten-year old? Was it that which lay at the heart of this need to discard the overlays of adulthood and social conditioning? Was I trying to strip myself back to the innocent boy I once was? The questions tumbled in, one after the other. Was there a link here too with the other prerequisite of my sailing – absolute simplicity? This was something which I had never considered before, but which seemed to make sense. I had always nurtured simplicity for its practical benefits, but now I began to see that it could have other, more metaphysical influences. Simplicity engenders purity, innocence. It is symptomatic of a world-view closer to that of the child rather than the hard-bitten, too-knowledgeable adult.

This was all quite startling. Was I becoming a kind of Parsifal – a pure fool, a holy innocent, and a wandering one at that? Well, there are worse options in this brief life.

A fat Brünnich's guillemot flew past, a long way from its probable home on Bear Island. The lone sea bird was a timely reminder that innocence is relative and that purity, for the truly self-aware, is unattainable.

11

We had been at sea for two weeks and the wind, for a while, had more or less abandoned us. In the all-enveloping grey we ghosted on, our movement through the limpid swell almost imperceptible. A veering headwind, such as it was, forced us to the east. We were going nowhere. Beneath us the water had shallowed to a mere five or six hundred metres, for here was a confluence of banks: the Schulz Bank, the Louise A. Boyd Bank, the Myreth Bank. By noon we had scraped over 74°North, putting us a hundred and eighty miles due west of Bear Island.

Thick fog caught hold of us once more and the wind expired. I lowered the sail and lashed the bundle tightly to the boom gallows. For ten hours or so we heaved gently to the untiring rhythm of the sea. A harbour porpoise lay on the surface and eyed us from astern.

An un-sailable movement of air from the north-west was replaced by its counterpart from the south-east, bringing fog yet again. At six-thirty the next morning I raised six, then seven panels, and achieved what might loosely be called forward motion in what might loosely be called a northerly direction. We overtook a plank of six-by-two timber bobbing on a mirrored surface. By seven-thirty the light smattering of catspaws had pitter-pattered off into the murk and so we languished once more. Not long afterwards a more muscular zephyr, still from the south-east, had us up and running once more. I calculated our speed at 5bpm – five bubbles per minute; not the most extravagant or serendipitous of paces, but a bubble is a bubble, and every one of them brought us closer to our goal.

With the bubbles came some unexpected sunshine and an almost clear horizon. I wondered for a moment whether we were finally entering the Arctic High but dismissed the idea as fanciful. The quality of the light and the dourly sub-Arctic geometry of the cloud formations were all wrong for that.

The wind gave up on us and I gave up on the wind. The fog returned. By noon we had somehow clawed out eighteen nautical miles over the previous twenty-four hours. A seal, with the look of an Atlantic Grey, popped its head up eighty yards off the starboard quarter. It was unusual to see one so far offshore. Its appearance reminded me that I had forgotten to buy a pinniped identification book – a careless oversight. A fulmar paddled along astern of us, keeping up with ease.

Wind and fog toyed with us for the rest of the day, going, coming, coming, going. A pitter-patter, of rain this time, brought me to the hatch. I wondered whether this precipitation might bring the promise of wind but after several minutes it stopped, harbinger of nothing but itself. The sea remained oil-smooth and there we lay, sometimes inching forward, sometimes causing a great din with the slatting of the sail, but getting nowhere for all that hoo-ha.

Our seeming immobility was of course an illusion. We may well have been stuck at a certain spot on the planet, but that spot was itself rotating at a rate of several thousand miles every twenty-four hours. I made some measurements on the chart and did some quick calculations. At 75°North, one degree of longitude is equal to seven minutes of latitude. The circumference of this line of latitude, which is also the distance any spot on it is rotating every twenty-four hours, therefore equals 360 x 7 = 2520 nautical miles. Our rate of rotation was therefore 2520 ÷ 24 = 105 miles an hour. We were not languishing at all; we were zipping around at a pretty cool ton. But that was only part of it – no more than our rate of spin. What about the speed at which we were orbiting that elusive sun? As far as I could recall that was nearly seventy thousand miles an hour. And the whole shebang was hurtling round the centre of our galaxy at something like half a million miles an hour. My head grew dizzy at the thought of all this gravitational joyriding. We were fizzing along. It is true that the fact that everything else seemed to be fizzing along in the same direction and at the same rate robbed our speed of a certain relativity, but why be confounded by mere appearance? *Mingming II* and I were not rooted to the spot – we were hurtling through space as merrily as the Starship Enterprise.

12

Before setting sail I had switched off my mobile phone and packed it away inside a small waterproof bag inside a bigger waterproof bag. That evening, just as I was dozing off, it began to ring. It took me a while to realise that the muffled tune came from my phone and even longer to find and open the appropriate bags. Normally my phone goes very quickly to answerphone but for some reason it kept on ringing and ringing. The screen was lit up. I did not have time to consider how it had managed to switch itself on or where its signal was coming from.

I pressed the answer button and held the phone to my ear. *Hello?*

Why you take so long to answer telephone? It was a woman's voice, somewhat shrill. She was shouting, as if trying to make herself heard from a long distance.

Who is this please?

Who is? Why you ask who is? Is Olga of course!

Olga?

Yes Olga! You no recognising? Is Olga beautiful daughter of very rich Russian oligarch you no rescuing from Bear Island last time you passing!

I vaguely remembered. There had been a message in a bottle; or at least I had conjectured thus, not actually having been able to retrieve the bottle.

Oh. Yes. Olga. How very nice to hear from you. How are you these days?

I no very happy Olga and still waiting you come rescue me!

Rescue you? But that was four years ago!

Yes, mister! Four years! Four years I waiting for good-breeding Englishman with very nice yacht and banking at Coutts but still you no coming!

Well, I really am awfully sorry, Olga. I've...er...been a bit busy.

Busy! You been bit busy! You come rescue me right now!

It's not as simple as that, Olga. I'm actually on an important expedition. I'm sure you are a very nice girl and everything but...er...

Hey, mister! You get your English ass over this way right now! I no care about stupid expedition! I want you rescue me!

Well, I...erm...that's very kind of you, Olga. I really am most touched. Perhaps I will give it some serious consideration.

Hey, mister! I very good Russian girl! Know plenty ways make old fart Englishman very hap...

The line went dead. I looked at the screen. The phone had switched itself off. There was no signal. I repacked it slowly and carefully in its protective bags and dozed off again, wondering why I never, ever, seemed to get these women out of my hair.

13

Just after midnight the wind swung right round to the south-south-west and began to blow hard. I made a temporary repair to an aft batten pocket. In the main it is not heavy weather which creates damage to the junk rig, but the heavy slatting caused by a mix of a very light wind and a lively sea. I had improved the system for keeping the more vulnerable upper battens in their pockets, using half inch stainless steel screws to ensure they did not work their way out of their webbing restraints. Now a lower batten end, which had been fine for the whole of the previous voyage, was starting to chew its way out of its pocket. Using the sharp tip of the knife on my multitool I scoured a hole in the carbon fibre batten and used light line to secure it and to tension the luff of the sail as best I could.

Once more the world was totally grey, although the horizon was clear. We had been at sea for sixteen days, and I began to think about how little wildlife I had seen. There were so many species which I would reasonably have expected to have observed during those two weeks, but so far had not: long-finned pilot whales, dolphins of various kinds, Iceland gulls, little auks, black guillemots, arctic skuas and so on. There even seemed to be far fewer fulmars; nor had I seen a single shearwater. There was no way I could determine whether this was all a matter of chance, exacerbated by the generally poor visibility we had so far encountered, or whether it was a result of a more fundamental decline in numbers. It certainly felt a little strange, almost unnatural, to see the sea and sky so empty.

We were by now less than sixty miles from 76°North, the line of latitude at which, in the past, we had emerged into the Arctic High. That afternoon, as the wind veered into the west, the cloud began to break up, the thick murk through which we had been sailing cleared off to the east, and for a short while I convinced myself that we were about to enter that state of summer grace known only at the ends of the earth. Having, it seemed, ridden the gauntlet of several weeks of fog and rain, my heart was ready for the change. I longed now to watch the sun trace its low parabola through the midnight sky; I yearned for the brilliance and clarity of an endless and sun-filled Arctic day.

It was not to be. Within less than an hour another band of heavy fog rolled in from the west, the wind slowly fell away, and by ten that evening we were once more becalmed, rolling gently to a smoothing sea.

Midnight came and it was now Thursday 19th July, our eighteenth day at sea. We may, for a short while, be going nowhere, but I was nonetheless immensely happy to be so far ahead of our original schedule. It was quite possible that by July 22nd, the day I had initially planned to set sail, we would already be at 80°North. Svalbard was now almost within striking distance; before too long we would be to the west of the Sørkapp, the South Cape.

The calm was short-lived and within a couple of hours we were up and running in a strengthening breeze from the east. Torrential rain scoured *Mingming II*'s now pristine decks. The wind got up to a Force 6 and we eased snugly north under a single panel. The heavy rain continued. I could not remember ever having rain this far north before. Fog joined the rain and the wind veered steadily to the south-east. I reduced sail to just half a panel, enough to keep us running easily towards Prins Karls Forland, now only eighty miles to our north-north-east. With land ahead my senses were on full alert. Outside, the nasty mix continued: fog, rain, a confused sea thrown up by the cold and shifting wind.

Foghorn! I assembled my little hand-held VHF radio, just in case. Two more blasts and the ship was gone; no doubt another *City of Scunthorpe*. It was eight-thirty in the evening, the time for dinner jackets, ball-gowns and the cha-cha-cha. The wind blew up more strongly from the south and I gybed to a more offshore tack; it was inimical, the idea of careering blindly towards a lee shore and the shallows of the Isfjord Bank. The wind eased a little and I reverted to our more landwards course. The fog cleared somewhat, revealing a hazy horizon, and the wind backed to south-east, a more favourable direction for our approach of the coast.

A check aft revealed a loose bolt through the tiller head. The nut had worked its way almost off the thread. I made only the second exit from the hatch to retighten it. During the operation, which interfered somewhat with the functioning of the self-steering gear, we inadvertently gybed and the mainsheet tore my glasses off. At sea I always have them attached to a lanyard round the back of my neck, which on this occasion probably stopped them from being whisked off into the Greenland Sea.

In fact, we were now pretty much into the Fram Strait, the stretch of water, about three hundred and fifty miles wide, separating Svalbard from Greenland. In the public psyche, mention of the *Fram* inevitably evokes associations with Nansen, but for me she is linked more closely to her sailing master, the great Norwegian seaman and explorer Otto Sverdrup, a man now largely lost to the long and dark shadows of time, but who was the epitome of Arctic excellence. It always warmed my heart to sail in the waters named for his ship.

14

We were advancing well, with a daily run of eighty-two nautical miles. Just before noon the first fin whale spout of the voyage fired off on our port quarter, further confirmation that we were now over the continental shelf. As if to underline the point there was a sudden blossoming of the previously absent wildlife: kittiwakes everywhere; a feeding frenzy of unidentified dolphins; a puffin making its habitual double circuit of the boat, wings going ten to the dozen to keep its undercarriage aloft; more dolphins; more kittiwakes; two more fin whales; two minke whales; Brünnich's guillemots zapping seawards and zipping landwards; little auks a-whirring.

We were closing the land quickly. By midnight just twenty-three miles of water lay between us and the stern cliffs of Prins Karls Forland. I began to realise that in my previous voyages to these parts I had been spoiled in the matter of landfalls. My mind swelled with a whole catalogue of magisterial headlands and needle peaks, all crisply illuminated under an azure sky, all pushing up slowly but surely above a clear-cut horizon, all just as they should be, just where they should be. I had almost discounted the possibility that it might not ever be thus. Nor had I considered the obvious fact that by keeping twelve miles offshore, in international waters, and thereby maintaining my liberty and integrity, I might not actually see a damned thing. Now, after several weeks of navigating through fog and fug, with every horizon draped about with an immutable haze, I began to wonder whether this might be the norm for the whole of this year's time in the High Arctic, and whether I may end up struggling to catch sight of so much as a distant insinuation of rock and ice.

I began to wonder too whether we had chanced upon some sort of Global Cloud Convention, held this year in the waters off Svalbard. Cloud seemed to be pouring in daily from all ends of the earth, here for its annual get-together. No doubt a full and exciting programme was planned, with seminars such as *Five Easy Ways to Improve Your Fog-Making Capability* and *Modern Methods for Greater Rain Creation*, and a full plenary session and debate on *The Geo-Politics of Cloud in a Changing Environment*. There was plenty of entertainment laid on too, the highlight, as ever, being the *Strictly Cloud Dance Competition*. This year's featured dance was, no doubt, the cha-cha-cha. I knew now why I had seen nothing but cloud jetting in from the south for week after week, stifling the sky hereabouts. It had seemed like every last cloud in the world was here, and indeed it was.

Under this constant sun-blocking pall I thought about the early navigators in these waters, the whalers and sealers and walrus-hunters who came up here every summer in their stout but rudimentary ships. How had they managed to navigate when overhead conditions were like this? We had gone for at least two weeks without a chance to obtain a meridian altitude, let alone work out, by celestial means, anything so luxurious as a longitude. Nor were we constrained or threatened by ice. They were of course wily seamen, the Dutch and Norwegian and British skippers of these northern fleets, and they had no doubt a catalogue of subtle clues and rules of thumb to find their way around, but all the same. The rewards for the annual slaughter could be huge, but the loss of life was considerable. Many a vessel, some of them no doubt lost and wandering uncertainly, was taken by the ice and never again seen.

The terrors of being trapped in the pack-ice are difficult to overstate. A ship did not lie there quietly, like a floating log frozen into the surface of a pond in winter. It was not a peaceful, static experience. The ice was in constant movement: heaving, squeezing, grinding, shrieking and wailing. The ship too, would soon become unstable, pressured upwards any old way, often creating a strong list to one side or the other, or lifting the bow or stern. The crew were in constant fear of a sudden sinking, and so had to be ready to abandon ship at any moment.

It is a strange fact that the discovery of Franz Josef Land itself was made by a ship thus trapped – the *Tegetthoff* – of the Austrian North Polar Expedition of 1872 – 1874. One of the joint leaders of the expedition, Julius Payer, describes the constant agony of entrapment[3]. It is January 26th 1873, as the ship, caught in the ice to the north-west of Novaya Zemlya, is carried inexorably north:

---

3   From *New Lands Within the Arctic Circle, Volume 1,* by Julius Payer, 1876, edition Forgotten Books, pages 224-5.

Scarcely asleep after the exhaustion and cares of the day, the timbers of the ship begin to moan and groan close by our ear, and we awake and lie listening to the onset of the ice. We hear the step of the watch on deck crackling on the ice as he paces to and fro; as long as it is measured and steady we know there is nothing to be feared. Again that uncanny creaking in the timbers and the watch comes to announce to those below that the terrible movement of the ice has begun, and once more we all spring from our beds, put on our fur clothes, seize our ready-filled bags, and amid the darkness stand ready on deck, and listen to the war between the ice and elements. In autumn, when the ice-fields were not nearly so large as in winter, their collision was accompanied by a deep dull sound; but now, rendered hard and brittle by the extreme cold, a sound of as a howl of rage was emitted as they crashed together. Ever nearer come the rushing, rattling sounds as if a thousand heavy wagons were driving over a plain. Close under us the ice begins to tremble, to moan and wail in every key; – as the fury of the conflict increases, the grumbling becomes deeper and deeper, concentric fissures open themselves round the ship, and the shattered portions of the floes are rolled up into heaps. The intermitting howls become fearfully rapid, announcing the acme of the conflict and anxiously we listen to the sound we know so well...Tables of ice broken off from the floes around us rise perpendicularly from the sea; some are bent under the enormous pressure, and their curved shapes attest to the elasticity of the ice...And in this wild and fearful tumult a ship – squeezed, pressed, all but crushed by the ice; her crew on deck, ready to leave her at a moment's notice.

THE " TEGETTHOFF " DRIFTING IN PACK-ICE --MARCH 1873.

The ship was eventually abandoned and her crew, an unlikely mix of Austrians, Hungarians and Croats, managed to make their way south with sledges and the ship's boats.

It was accounts like this that put my own Arctic meanderings into some sort of perspective. I was up there for little more than a pleasant and relatively undemanding summer jaunt. Satellite technology gave me a pretty accurate preview of how the ice lay; it enabled me too to fix my position at any time of the day or night to within a few yards of accuracy. The land hereabouts was comprehensively mapped, the ocean well sounded. I was under no pressure to produce any kind of result: to get anywhere in particular; to discover anything new; to meet the expectations of backers and compatriots. I was just out for an extended day sail – Whitehills and back; where I went was entirely up to me.

Nonetheless, it was important to me to try to grasp, as best I could, a sense of how it must have felt to have been amongst the firstcomers to these high latitudes. In one respect I had something in common with them: if I ran into trouble I would have to shift for myself. I had no means of calling for help, nor would I ever have wanted one. I was there of my own volition and for my own entirely selfish, or at least self-centred, purposes. It was fundamental to the underlying philosophy of these voyages that I be entirely self-sufficient. To have an artificial safety net of any kind, beyond what I had built into the construction and management of the boat, would have negated and destroyed the very essence of what I was doing. It would have compromised the absolute purity of the conception; one man, one boat, one sail.

I did not delude myself, however, that this made me anything of an explorer, or even much of an adventurer. I was little more than a stubborn old fool who occasionally liked going off for a long sail in unfrequented waters.

15

With a fresh wind mainly from the south-east, and further helped by a strong northerly current, we were still haring along. Once again we made well over eighty miles noon to noon. Our progress was almost too rapid: no land had yet been sighted in the continuing fog and rain, and we risked leaving Prins Karls Forland astern, unseen. Seven years previously we had lain off the island in a regal calm, studying at leisure its peaks and glaciers, and all the while gyrating lazily north on the last remnants of the Gulf Stream. Perhaps unreasonably, I had anticipated a rerun of those heady moments.

I decided to alter course to a more landward heading, in the hope of uncovering the Fuglehuken, the northern tip of Prins Karls Forland. Beyond this point the Svalbard mainland lay further to the east, its coastline on a north-south axis. I wanted to keep as close a contact as I dared, in order to take advantage of any lifting of the engulfing pall. Our noon position put us just seven and a half miles from the Fuglehuken, but nothing was visible. This was scarcely surprising, for we would probably have had to approach the coast within less than a mile to have had any chance of seeing it.

Rain squalls, each one heavier than the last, came in and drummed tattoos on the cabin roof. A black guillemot flew round the boat and landed just off the port quarter with an ungainly flop of its rotund belly. The fog thickened, the rain drummed harder, the sky darkened. I sat in the half-light below, listening to the roar of the rain overhead, and boiled water for a mug of hot bouillon. It was the only remedy I could think of to relieve our total suffocation.

I drank the scalding liquid and carefully rearranged my mindset. We had been at sea for almost three weeks now, and I had allowed my expectations to swell to a disproportionate and irrational stature. I knew well enough that hope and expectation are the destroyers of tranquillity, but a slackening of mental discipline on my part had allowed them to gain a temporary ascendency. I wrote a short note in my personal log, reminding myself that the principle is not to have any regard for how things might have been, or once were, or could be again, but simply to accept and deal with things exactly as they are.

Later that afternoon a beguiling patch of lighter sky pushed low over the horizon to the south-west. I ignored it. There was no point exercising my imagination as to what it might or might not herald.

A small merchant ship passed us two miles on our starboard beam, heading south, the first vessel we had seen for several weeks. The sky, which had been showing signs of relenting a little, grew threatening once more and a huge rain cloud passed astern. The wind strengthened and I reduced sail to just a single panel. It was nearly midnight and I turned in for an hour's sleep.

At one thirty in the morning of Sunday 22nd July, our twenty-first day at sea, I woke to a changed world. I surveyed the scene, astonished by the speed and comprehensiveness of the transition, uplifted by the stark beauty of the uncovered land, and immeasurably happy that at last we had found some reward for the hard slog of the previous few weeks.

Overhead was a sky now patterned with great tracts of pale blue and interspersed with high strata of coppery and almost immobile cloud. For the first time of the voyage the light had that indefinable Arctic quality, a kind of metallic glow, burnished and otherworldly. For the moment the air had rid itself of the heavy moisture which had clung about us for weeks, leaving, to the west, a crystalline horizon, and to the east, laid out north to south in perfect clarity, the mountains of Albert 1 Land, the north-west region of Spitsbergen. Way astern, on our starboard quarter, the dark mass of the Fuglehuken rose tall and narrow, revealed at last.

The Peaks of NW Spitsbergen, from NW c. 12 miles

The mountains of Albert 1 Land, a tight-packed jumble of razor-sharp and jagged ridges and incisors thrusting skywards from their connecting snowfields and glaciers, defy adequate description. The spikey summits, all of a muchness as regards altitude, are uncountable. The topography, at first sight, suggests chaos, anarchy, insane randomness, but this is an illusion created by its sheer unlikeliness. In fact there is an underlying cohesion in the way the patterning of the peaks and valleys repeats itself for mile after mile, north to south, west to east. The land here has been subject to the same forces and has reacted uniformly, creating a startling and repetitive mosaic of black rock and sparkling ice.

Just one peak has the temerity to rise above the rest and dominate: the Kaffitoppen, a sharp and pyramidal Matterhorn of a mountain, thrusting high above its fellow summits, and therefore dominating the skyline from every direction. Here and there shafts of sunlight illuminated portions of the range, throwing the deeply cleft ridges and arêtes into sharp relief and infusing the inter-lying icefields with a soft glow. It was a pied landscape of black on white, with every horizontal line crazily jagged, cutting air and ice with saw-toothed ferocity.

It was worth the long haul just to spend a single hour contemplating these silent pinnacles; even at this early stage of the voyage I already knew that I would go home a happy man. Here was the wildness I sought laid out in uncompromising solidity; here one could grasp, just a little, the age and indifference of the earth, of pure and inanimate matter going about its business for aeon after aeon. I tried to picture the slow dissolution of these mountains, their crumbling and erosion and gradual softening. One day they might be nothing but low and rolling hills; perhaps, eventually, they will fall back below the surface of the sea whence they came. I was happy to have caught them, as it were, at the moment of their extravagant grandeur, at the very apex of their sharpness and vitality. It was nothing but the intersection of two disparate lifelines: my own, absurdly brief but weighed down by sentience; theirs, long beyond imagining but untroubled by mind. The paradox was that there was no great difference in our essential matter. We were just different arrangements of the same fundamental molecules. There was no inherent separateness – pretty much everything was potentially transferable. Everything, that is, except my own fragile life force.

Here too was another paradox: it was in the contemplation of these dead-cold peaks that I felt more alive than ever. Their lifeless frigidity infused me with a great warmth. It would be untrue to say that my pulse beat more strongly, but every nerve end seemed to tingle; my senses were heightened to a penetrating intensity. It was impossible for me to reciprocate the magnificent indifference of those black mountains, for they set something racing inside me, something beyond my control. I was at the mercy of their strange beauty. I knew that this reaction was irrational, but there was nothing I could do about it.

I tacked landwards, drawn in towards the line of glaciers funnelling down into the sea, broad white tracts of ice approaching their own particular form of dissolution and death.

16

A cruise ship appeared, heading north several miles inshore of us; another sea-going conurbation eating up the miles with absurd ease. It was blue-hulled, this one, with the standard white superstructure of all such vessels, deck piled on deck, up and up, and crowned with an assortment of white spheres and domes housing, no doubt, an array of technological wizardry. It seemed to be angling in towards the land, heading perhaps for Danksøya, the island at the north-west tip of Spitsbergen, of which more a little later.

The ship purred off north with feline smoothness, leaving me once more to my own crude devices. The wind was coming off and at four-thirty I dropped and lashed the sail. I had found the mountains and the calm I had hungered for and so was happy to be going nowhere, drifting idly along on a faint current and disturbed by no more than the occasional bickering of our accompanying fulmars.

I thought about the last time I was off this coast in notionally similar circumstances. At that point, having arrived via Jan Mayen, we were near the end of our northerly trajectory. All that had remained was to see if we could push on as far as 80°North, only another sixty miles or so. The ice conditions that year had been vastly different; I was still something of a tyro, too, at such high latitudes, and so was advancing tentatively, unsure of what to expect. This time it felt as if the voyage had only just begun. Our arrival off Albert 1 Land marked the end of the first stage only. 80°North was now nothing but a waypoint from which to begin the real business of the enterprise. In the years between the two voyages my mental conceptions had been completely realigned. The stratum of high latitudes in which it seemed possible and acceptable to navigate had moved firmly north. Where 80°North had once seemed to be the absolute limit, it was now the base line. If I conceived of any reasonable limit, it was now 82°North. I was still, therefore, confined within a northern boundary, albeit much higher. On the other hand, if I could successfully weather the most northerly point of Svalbard, I would open up a run of clear water to the east which even four years earlier had seemed unattainable. When I was here in 2011 I was sailing into a narrowing vector, the apex of a tall triangle; this time I was close to opening up a whole new and spacious expanse in which to navigate. I was tingling, therefore, with quiet anticipation. We had sailed more than fifteen hundred miles already, but the real business of the voyage still lay far to the north and even further to the east.

This short-lived calm provided an ideal hiatus in which to take stock and gear myself mentally for the next, perhaps most critical, stage of the circuit. I was able to spend some time, too, photographing, filming and sketching the singular landscape of Albert 1 Land. I still held the office of President (and Sole Member) of the Distant Glacier Photographic Society, and so felt duty-bound to capture the best possible images of the array of icy tongues clogging the valleys between the mountain shoulders. The results were of the usual poor quality, but there was little I could do about it. When becalmed, a boat is still in constant motion, even if rolling only very gently; this is enough to preclude the use of long lenses. Moreover, the softness of the light at that hour of the morning demanded longer exposure times. It was impossible, therefore, to produce sharp, close-up images of particular features. All I could do was to take wide, general shots. Even using my best prime lens on my number one camera, these were never of the kind of crisp quality I would have liked. I had long since reconciled myself to the fact that given my defensive strategies, which mostly kept us well offshore, I would only rarely capture decent images. Ultimately this was a trade-off I was prepared to make; it was more important to navigate as prudently as possible than to take good photographs.

At eight that morning a breeze came in from the east-north-east and we got under way again with four panels set. After a predominantly downwind passage from Whitehills it felt good to be back to some honest windward work, sailing due north full and bye. In lighter airs anyway I prefer to have the wind forward of the beam. The apparent wind is increased, the self-steering gear is happier and *Mingming II* can exhibit her fine windward balance.

Little Ayls

Only one development marred the morning: a mass of moisture-laden air was rolling up from the south, blotting out the mountains as it came. I felt more sanguine about the approaching mist, having been able to spend a number of hours absorbing every detail of the landscape. We were into the High Arctic proper and north-west Spitsbergen had been revealed as clearly as I could have hoped. I could allow myself to relax a little.

We ranged on easily, always to the north, and by noon were just three miles from 80°. My mind brimmed with vivid recollections of my last foray to this latitude – a quick dart to that heady point in a steady north-westerly; a sky hung with long veils of diaphanous purple cloud; a sea dotted to the horizon with little auks and the occasional black guillemot; my own near-disbelief that I was there in nothing but a tiny, light-limbed Corribee.

A gentle rain began to fall and before long we were once more engulfed in thick fog. At twelve fifty-five we crossed 80°North and so, for the first time on this voyage, entered new territory. It was Sunday 22nd July. In 2011 I had arrived here on the 24th July. Less than ten miles lay between the two crossing points.

17

I have rarely felt so joyful at sea. With the wind easing, and *Mingming II* now regal under the full spread of her sail, all seven panels arching skywards, we ghosted smoothly north. The sea and its attendant mist glowed with burnished silver, overlaying the moment with a patina of enchantment.

I sat in the hatchway, somehow liberated, released, intoxicated by a mix of intense aliveness and searing fulfilment. It seemed as if half a century of sailing had been no more than a preparation for this instant in time. Everything now made sense. I could feel, viscerally, as deep down in the pit of my stomach as it was possible to penetrate, the reasons for and the rightness of the stripped-down voyaging I had been honing for so long. It was not enough just to go somewhere; it only made sense to go somewhere under the strictest constraints of input. Here we were, slicing gently north in almost unsounded, almost unsailed waters, not in some fancy off-the-shelf leviathan, but in a modest little boat bought as a wreck and painstakingly reconstructed just, it seemed, for this very moment. During the several years of that reconstruction I of course had no idea where we might end up; what I was creating was a means, a set of possibilities, a platform for self-expression and for self-examination. The superficial quirkiness of the boat and its rig belied the uncompromising logic and discipline which had been applied to its reconstruction. Its final form had grown organically from its strict preconditions: strength, simplicity and ease of management. I had thought about these things for many years and laboured hard and long to bring it all to this final expression, to a kind of apotheosis.

Now was the moment of reward for all that labour. Moisture welled in my eyes; my throat felt tight. I looked up and examined the sail, every last stitch of it sewn by my own hand. Here it was, carrying us effortlessly to the very edge of the possible. I looked at the mast, a fine upstanding spar, reassuring in its girth and solidity, and remembered the day when it was unloaded off its delivery lorry, a forty-five foot municipal lamp post ripe for readjustment and an unpremeditated career. My heart swelled at the sight of *Mingming II's* decks and coach roof, scoured bright by three weeks of wind and sea, uncluttered, unflexing, unfailingly watertight; all this the result of months and months of minutely detailed refurbishment.

There was no specific aim in mind during those hard years of reconstruction. All I knew was that it had to be done; that if I could do it, and do it as well as I knew how, then the rest would follow. Perhaps this could be construed as an act of faith, but I never envisaged it that way. I was old enough and aware enough to appreciate the power of logic and causality; I knew that as long as I made the best possible job of it, then B would follow A, and C would follow B as surely as the sun rises day after day.

The voyage I was engaged on was of course a continuum, an endless flow of moments, each running into the next, and in that sense had no real culmination. Nonetheless, as we carried on sailing past 80°North and as I sat in the hatchway in a state of heightened receptivity, I felt that I had reached a kind of apex, not simply geographically, but in terms of a lifetime's sailing and its meaning. By crossing 80°North and sailing on and on, we had somehow transgressed, not simply into the realm of the abnormal, but into of the world of the unthinkable. For a little while I felt light-headed, light-bodied, almost devoid of corporeal substance. I hesitate to use the word *rapture*, with its quasi-religious overtones, but the intensity of my happiness and sense of arrival might thus be expressed. Over the years I had experienced many moments of deep and penetrating euphoria while at sea, but nothing matched the feeling of those few hours.

For a while I was possessed of an overwhelming urge to keep on sailing north, to keep going, on and on, until stopped by the edge of the pack-ice, or an agglomeration of floes too dense to sail through. This was somewhat more than a mere mischievous fancy. The desire to throw all caution aside and execute a kind of magnificently foolhardy flourish, a glorious and possibly terminal throw of the dice, took a strong grip on my imagination and for a while refused to let go. In my disembodied, somewhat floaty state I was easy prey for such a seductive and romantic notion. *Just keep going, sunshine! Who knows? You might get to eight-two north before you hit anything!* The soft leading wind, if it held, was perfect for such a madcap scheme, it being always better to approach danger upwind, the easier to turn and escape quickly should any nastiness arise. The sea was smooth and unthreatening. What's more, my chart stopped at 81° 30'. That in itself added more temptation by creating another delicious notion – to sail right off the chart, off onto the white margin, as it were, of an area already unsullied by such mundane and temporal things as soundings, and then off the margin itself and into the silver void beyond.

For a long time I wrestled with that temptation, the ensuing battle-royal symbolic of my own duality: on the one hand the incurable but subversive romantic, on the other hand the hard-nosed, disciplined ascetic. The former longed to make that outrageous gesture, and hang the consequences; the latter, more distanced and objective, argued hard against the risks to the greater enterprise. Looking back, I can see now that what was playing out was the age-old dichotomy inherent in adventuring. An adventurer must have, *a priori*, a strong romantic and therefore irrational streak, but a successful adventurer must also be firmly grounded in rational practicality. To lean too far towards the former is to invite catastrophe; too much of the latter might well deter the prospective swashbuckler completely, inviting him rather to stay at home and tend his roses. Somewhere between the two extremes lies a happy medium that encourages adventure, but also restrains it from exuberantly optimistic excess.

To the south, the mist was clearing, revealing once more the north-west corner of Spitsbergen. From our new vantage point I could see the two islands that lie close to the end of the mainland, Amsterdamøya and Danskøya, and the narrow north-south passage that separates them from the mountains of Albert 1 Land. Danskøya figures large in the history of polar exploration, its associations serving as a warning against the kind of blind optimism that I was at that moment attempting to subdue. In 1897 the Swedish scientist and explorer Salomon Andrée had launched his hydrogen balloon from Danskøya in a madcap scheme to fly to the North Pole. He and his two companions perished, unsurprisingly, without ever having made any significant northing. What happened to Andrée and his crew remained one of the great mysteries of the early twentieth century until 1930, when the detritus of the expedition, complete with notebooks, was found on the island of Kvitøya, two hundred miles to the east. Andrée's case illustrates as well as any the fine and shifting line that divides heroism from stupidity. It also points up the corrosive power of self-publicity when applied to the sphere of adventure. In some ways Andrée was an earlier example of a Donald Crowhurst figure. Like Crowhurst, his own misplaced enthusiasm and pronouncements drove him into a corner from which there was no escape; he talked himself into having no choice but to engage on a venture for which he was under-prepared both technically and in terms of relevant experience.

Andrée was at least a trained scientist, but his successor on Danskøya, the American Walter Wellman, was little more than a hustling ex-newspaperman. Wellman, who had begun his career reporting on polar exploration, before realising that there was more potential for fame and fortune inherent in being the actual explorer, had led a chaotic and spectacularly unsuccessful expedition to Franz Josef Land. Relieved of his duties by the new sponsor of American exploration in that region, the ageing baking powder magnate William Ziegler, Wellman, like Andrée, began to dream up airborne schemes for getting to the Pole. Wellman had tried without success to get himself aboard Andrée's balloon. Between 1906 and 1909 Wellman used Danskøya as his base for three attempts to reach the North Pole using a motor-powered airship. In 1906 the engines self-destructed when tested on the ground; in 1907 he covered fifteen miles; in 1909 he covered sixty miles to the north before a line holding essential ballast broke, causing him to turn round and seek a tow from a Norwegian survey ship.

Sobered up by recollections of these cautionary tales still hanging heavy in the air above Danskøya, I re-focussed on the essential business of the moment – the weathering of the Sjuøyane, the Seven Islands, the last northern outposts of Svalbard. With the wind, such as it was, settling into the east-north-east I had the prospect of a long haul to windward. Later that afternoon I went about and headed south-east, back towards the line of rugged peaks lying low on the southern horizon. For the moment, at any rate, I had deflected the siren call to the north. Sometimes I wonder whether I ought to have carried on. Even now it is a seductive thought.

18

The wind soon died, and for a while I let *Mingming II* drift along freely under her full sail, not so much moving as revolving and evolving, like the masses of Arctic cloud overhead. These never seemed to exhibit any progress in any definable direction, but were nonetheless in a constant flux, changing their form and consistency by the minute. Clear patches of sky were lost in a few seconds to strata of cloud that seemed to materialise out of nothing; conversely, cloud would suddenly melt into nowhere to reveal patches of hazy and bronze-tinted blue.

Another cruise ship passed to the south of us, several miles away, and made off in an unlikely direction – the north-west. Maybe it was heading for the top of Greenland. For a while I could just make out the intrusive rumble of its engines, no more than a faint undertone, but enough to threaten the wholesome silence in which we were now immersed. The ship was soon lost over the grainy horizon, leaving us in sole possession of all the wilderness hereabouts, and its total peace. It was the last vessel I would see for several weeks.

Just after seven in the evening I lowered and lashed the sail. We drifted on to the north-east, pushed almost imperceptibly, even at this high latitude, by the final remnants of the Gulf Stream. I sat in the hatchway, watching the land unfold to our south-east, with suggestions of distant headlands and ice cliffs pushing through the soft evening light.

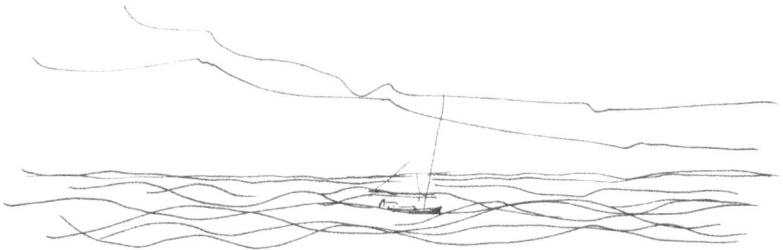

Becalmed

Three puffins arrived and spent half an hour paddling around the boat, examining every detail. At first I kept myself well hidden in the hatchway, thinking that I might otherwise scare them off, but I soon learned that they were without fear. My presence and movements as I photographed them in no way unnerved them. They were by far the tamest puffins I have ever encountered. Maybe this was the first small boat they had ever seen; maybe I was the first man they had ever seen. Their guileless trust was heart-warming, as was their occasional exchange of quiet, throaty grunts.

I have of course seen thousands of puffins over the years, but never so close. I tried to conceive of the evolutionary path that had led to such an extraordinary manifestation of life. The black and white markings around their faces, and particularly their eyes, topped as they are with a tall but tiny triangle of black eye shadow, have an exquisite subtlety that gives them a permanently surprised, questioning and somewhat doleful look. It is the coloration of their bills, though, that is, in its own way, wondrous. How and why did such a multi-pigmented pattern evolve, with its mix of orange-reds, creamy-yellows and blue-blacks? And why the baroque shape, compared to the more standardised bills of the other auks? This outrageous palette and extravagant architecture seemed more fitting for the tropical jungle than the monochrome wastes of the Arctic. Well, evolution, we are told, is a trail of infinite experiments along infinite paths, some long-lived, some short-lived with most, if not all, ultimately doomed to failure. It is unlikely that puffins will, in the long run of geological time, survive, but for the moment they cannot fail at least to raise a smile. The irony is that they themselves are unaware of their comical beauty.

Sated by what seemed to be their first close brush with civilisation, the puffins eventually left us, whirring away towards the land and more important business. I was a little sad to see them go; theirs was the kind of company of which I could never tire. There was so much to learn from them. Those little birds, with their clown-like innocence were, in almost every way, much better creatures than I.

A slight breeze came up from the north-east but I ignored it, preferring sleep to dickering around making no progress to windward. Another puffin made a quick visit and a small seal, perhaps one of the harbour seals that live at Danskøya, studied us from various angles.

It was now the early morning of Monday 23rd July, so we were nearing the end of our third week at sea. All night and all morning we lay there, sometimes in the flattest of calms, sometimes caressed by a faint but impractical breath from the north-north-east. The north coast of Spitsbergen stretched out to the east, beckoning, but for the moment unreachable. I had hoped, if possible, to pass close to the circular reef known as Moffen, which lies a dozen miles or so off the coast. It is home to a large colony of walruses, and so may have enabled me to make up for the single brief encounter I had during my previous Arctic voyage. Tilman had sailed past Moffen on his way to the Hinlopen Strait fifty years earlier, and the strange name of this strange island had been imprinted on my consciousness for decades.

Noon came. We had covered just twenty-three miles. A few spots of rain heralded thickening cloud. A muscular swell came in from the south-west, setting us rolling. We managed to sail for an hour or so on our south-easterly tack, but round about three in the afternoon the rain came on more strongly and the wind once more faded. A black guillemot flew past, all sagging belly and whishing wings. Once more I dropped and lashed the sail and stretched out on my bunk, listening to the rain splattering the coach roof.

It is like that so often in the High Arctic summer: a constant round of stop and start, of harnessing gutless respirations from here and there. It demands infinite patience and philosophical robustness. The man who is always in a hurry would be better to stay at home. Snug under my unzipped sleeping bag and a blanket or two, I lay on my back and dozed on and off. I could see, through the after portlight, the ship's ensign hanging limply from the topmost sheet of the furled sail. I had long since learned that if it flaps occasionally there is no point budging; a sailing breeze keeps the tattered little flag constantly at the horizontal. With my infallible wind gauge thus visible at the opening of half an eye, I had no need to bestir myself unnecessarily. This was not a question of laziness, but of culling the maximum benefit from my haphazardly spaced rest periods. In the Arctic summer that psychological inducement to sleep – darkness – is permanently absent, upsetting the circadian rhythm and further disrupting the already disrupted sleep patterns of the singlehanded sailor. If sleep would not come, then the next best thing was to lie quietly with closed eyes.

At eight that evening the ensign started to show signs of life. Soon there was enough of a breeze to keep it stretched out horizontally, and so I once again raised the sail, all seven panels of it, and resettled us to the same course, the wind still holding in the east-north-east. I had no faith in this new incarnation of the same old headwind and was preparing my mind for a protracted period of stop-start and painfully slow windward work. In principle this did not bother me at all; I was happy to sail in whatever conditions we met. It did, however, restrict the lines available to us on our port and starboard tacks, making it impossible, for the moment, to follow the east-north-east slanting coastline with an easy parallel course. Whether our fitful working into and away from the coast would bring us close to Moffen was something of an open question.

In fact I had underestimated this new wind. Not only did it strengthen, forcing us, by midnight, down to four panels, but it also veered into the east. At three in the morning I tacked, for we now had a leading wind, a wind that if it held would allow us to weather the Seven Islands on a single board. A massive squall of black cloud loomed up an hour or two later, and there we were down to a panel and a half, plunging on to the north-east with rain once more thrumming on the coach roof. I had hardly slept all night and for once relented on my rule of not allowing sleep between breakfast and lunch.

It was, while it lasted, a bounteous wind, but as the morning progressed it began to dwindle away. By eleven-thirty we were once more becalmed. Our noon position put us at 80° 21'North. Over the previous twenty-four hours we had made good just twenty-two nautical miles, noon position to noon position. To achieve that modest distance we had in fact sailed thirty-eight miles in all. Such is windward work. With eighty miles or so still to cover in order to reach Ross Island, the most northerly of the islands, and the terrestrial limit of Western Europe, there was still much to do. Well, there was no hurry. With the Svalbard coastline laid out west to east thirty miles to our south there was plenty to look at and to contemplate. Most importantly, though, I had not seen the slightest indication of any sea ice. I could see no reason why, with patience, we would not manage to make our passage around the northern extremity of Svalbard.

19

We are lucky indeed to have been born onto a planet where the wind blows, and whose surface is mostly clothed in that restless, mysterious amniotic fluid we call the sea. Of all the infinite possible combinations of matter and motion, what better conjunction could ever be imagined? What other combination could yield so much possibility?

Above, we have currents of air that most of the time move along within a benign range, their energy easily harnessed by no more than a few square feet of sailcloth. Outside of that range, tolerable calms are more common than intolerable hurricanes. Most of the time, then, and in most places, the winds are sailable. Moreover, the rotating nature of weather systems lends enough variety to the direction of the wind as to make any destination possible. Some routes are more favourable than others, of course, as are some seasons, but in principle, ice-bound regions excepted, any point on land can be reached from any other under sail alone. Before the arrival of mechanical power, it was wind and sail that enabled the full exploration of the planet; oar-powered craft could only go so far and of course lost their effectiveness in anything of a sea.

It takes an incalculable number of subtle and varying phenomena and factors to produce winds which sit most of the time within their benign range for navigation: the density and depth of the atmosphere, the varying heat of the sun, the warming and cooling of the sea and of the land, the circumference and the rate of rotation of the planet, and so on, each one of these open to infinite analysis. The balance between these wind-controlling phenomena is finely tuned and quite possibly fragile. Having known nothing else, we take the generally friendly winds to which we are subject for granted, as if it could never be otherwise. Think for a second or two of Neptune, where the winds blow at twelve hundred miles per hour.

And what about the invisibility of the air; the fact that although it is matter, as anyone trying to stand on a clifftop in a Force Ten wind will attest, we can see right through it? We know the scientific reasons for this, but it seems to be yet another happy coincidence. Here we have a powerful motive force, but one which does not obscure our vision, or one for which, to an extent, our vision has evolved in such a way as not to be obscured by it.

Then there is the sea itself, its basic components molecules of gases combined and transformed, by a most improbable sleight of hand, into a fluid medium. There is something almost miraculous about this fluidity, pliant enough to be easily displaced but resistant enough to support an appropriate structure. Imagine if the sea had the consistency of engine oil or honey. Once again the parameters seem to have fallen within an ideal range. This does not discount the possibility that had things been arranged otherwise, different techniques might have been developed to harness their potential, or that we may have evolved differently to cope with them, but the fact remains that the combination of generally benign wind and hydrodynamically compliant sea is so rare and unlikely, when viewed from a universal perspective, that every sailor ought to make a daily and devout libation to whatever gods or causes he or she deems responsible for this state of affairs.

For there is nothing on this planet, nothing whatsoever, comparable to sailing its oceans. Nothing else can take a man so far, into so many varied and obscure regions of the globe, entirely on his own terms but with so little input of internal or external energy. Nothing else gives him so much freedom of movement. In no other enterprise can he remain in motion, totally self-sufficient, for so long. In no other way can a man disassociate himself so comprehensively, if he so wishes, from anything even remotely reminiscent of normal, land-borne existence; nothing else can bring him so uncompromisingly face to face with an alien and elemental Nature. The closest parallel is, I think, climbing high mountains, but I have done both and find the comparison ultimately untenable. There is simply no greater apartness and primal vulnerability to be found than that of being a thousand miles offshore in a raging storm.

Few things, too, can match the beauty of the conception. The media of wind and water impose forms on sail and hull which, at their best expression, can reach an aesthetic pinnacle. That aesthetic is founded on the sweetly curved line: the longitudinal and transverse curves of the hull; the subtle sweep of a well-drawn sheer-line; the incisive curvature of a judiciously cut sail. Added to that is the heeling of the craft, sometimes gentle, sometimes extreme, but always reducing the rigidity of the notional right angle between mast and surface, and imparting an aliveness and sinuousness into the motion that no powered vessel can ever match. I recalled the sleek and sweetly lined Dutch yacht I had seen powering to windward towards Shetland, her innate beauty negated by her nakedly aggressive and upright stance, her total lack of harmony with either wind or wave.

I thought, too, about the almost inevitable fusion of the aesthetic with the utilitarian. It seems that clarity of purpose, however mundane, or even murderous, somehow invites purity of form. There are few vessels afloat, for example, as heart-stopping as an Essex smack under full sail, or a Thames barge, or a trading dhow, or a Chinese junk. And what of the old ships-of-the-line? Imagine *HMS Victory* with all her canvas set, all six and a half thousand square yards of it, her three and a half thousand tons of displacement driven at eight knots by this astounding acreage of curving cloth. I tried to work out why naked functionality seems to converge with expressive form, why the tension between the two so often resolves into something so powerful, something transcendent of the underlying prosaicness.

My own heart and eyes were biased, of course, but I had always found something felicitous in *Mingming II*'s crude utilitarianism. She was re-built uncompromisingly for a specific purpose, with no thought whatsoever for visual appeal, except for an unsubtle harmonisation of her overall colour scheme of black combined with several shades of grey. The guiding principles were no more than strength and total practicality. Her angular, straight-sided observation pod, for example, which along with her sail is her most striking feature, was constructed purely with indestructibility and ease of assembly in mind. I wondered whether whatever beauty *Mingming II* may possess (allowing that many may find her just plain ugly) was to be found in this nakedly functional form itself, or whether her appeal was secreted in what that form may subliminally suggest: adventure, non-conformism and an anachronistic rejection of advanced technology. Perhaps it was a mix of both.

Whatever the answer may be, I felt an unbounded gratitude that the life which had come my way, unasked for and still largely uncomprehended, had graced me with this triple bounty: wind, sea and a boat to sail. For the moment, though, there was no sailing to be done. I finished my lunch of rye bread, cheese and an apple, and stretched out on my bunk. *Mingming II* waltzed gently around, animated by no more than a faint and easing swell from the north-east.

20

After just a short while a muscular little wind came in from the north-west. It was a breeze which, had it held, would have allowed us to range at will along that northerly coast. We could, perhaps, have sailed in close to Moffen and seen for ourselves whether the tales of great colonies of walrus were true; we may have been able to sail across the mouth of the Hinlopen Strait and looked down its length, thinking of Tilman and his trials at its southern end; we would, in short, have had a freedom of movement that had so far been denied. It was a cold wind, which brought heavy rain with it, but it was as fickle, and ultimately as short-lived, as the rest.

Throughout the night we were taunted by squalls of lashing rain interspersed with promises of clearer sky to the north-west. The wind dropped right down and then revived itself, forcing a severe reduction of sail. It backed a little towards the west and I started to run in towards the land, ever the optimist. It was a fading wind, though, and with the swell from the north-east still enough to roll *Mingming II* from side to side, the sail and its battens were slatting with a maddening squeal and thump. I was forever at the hatchway adjusting this and that: the mainsheet, the steering gear, the amount of sail set; searching always for the optimum settings; squeezing whatever I could out of the uncongenial conditions. For it must be said that sailing is not always a graceful and beauteous progress through silky seas. From time to time, with the wrong sea and the wrong wind, it becomes plain ugly, to be endured rather than savoured. Such was this night, which ran me ragged with its incessant demands and its ceaseless cacophony.

Just before five in the morning everything changed. Within just a minute or two the breeze swung right round to the south-east, bringing us once more hard on the wind and forcing us away from the coast. Moffen and the Hinlopen Strait were now beyond easy reach, but there was one consolation: if this wind held it would bring us, on this starboard tack alone, directly to Ross Island and the end of the land. There was another consoling feature too: carving easily to windward under six panels of sail, we were done with the crashing and whining of a slatting rig. Peace and harmony were now restored, beauty reinstated. The sky was clearing too, the cloud driven off by fresher, clearer air. I breakfasted early and took a short nap.

Now thirty miles off the coast, with an offshore wind, the sea empty of the least possibility of traffic, and no indication of any ice hereabouts, I slept a deep and easy sleep. I had little doubt now that anything could frustrate our first objective – the weathering of northern Svalbard. For an hour or so I fell into a reviving slumber, smoothing out the disruptions of the previous night, readying my mind for the day ahead. I wanted to be fresh and in a state of maximum receptivity, both to enjoy the moment and to enable it to imprint itself indelibly on my neural circuits. Viewed objectively, it was a small thing: another passage round another rock in another patch of the planet's ocean. It brought no value to man or beast, contributed nothing to civilisation, required only a modicum of skill and determination. It was no big deal; in the great scheme of things it was meaningless, frivolous, supremely self-indulgent. Subjectively, though, it had the potential to be the highpoint of a lifetime's sailing. It was a big deal for me personally. Within the narrow context of my own psyche it did have meaning, both in itself and metaphorically. It enhanced the structure of my own life-story, helping to make sense of it, giving it shape, simultaneously unravelling and synthesizing the many threads of seventy years of often pained and painful existence into a satisfying dénouement. If the injunction of the philosopher is first to know yourself, to put your own house in order, then it was not totally without merit, for I sensed that if I could accomplish the small tasks of this voyage, I might be led a little closer to tranquillity. Although strictly personal, maybe even this was not without some tiny but nonetheless positive wider benefit; perhaps the only thing that a man can do to counteract the shrill enervation of post-modern civilisation is to promote his own calmness.

The more I thought about it as I lay on my bunk, now awake and fizzing with energy for the day ahead, the more I began to understand the metaphorical power of the high latitudes. For well over a decade I had lost all interest in what might be termed west-east, or east-west sailing. An Atlantic crossing, for example, especially via the southern route, held no appeal whatsoever. My drive was always principally to cut across, rather than follow, the lines of latitude. As luck would have it, my chosen north-south trajectory lay pretty much on the Greenwich meridian. That was the line that attracted me. To sail north along 0° longitude was to find the quickest route to both wilderness and self-knowledge. And in both of those lay danger and the unknown. There was a great appeal too in that zero of the Greenwich longitude: 0°. Although an arbitrary construct, it was nonetheless the no-man's-land between east and west, an infinitesimal nothingness. Like millions of others, I have stood astride the meridian at the Greenwich observatory, thereby straddling the two longitudinal hemispheres, one foot in each, the body divided between occident and orient. Now, in my own yacht, I could follow that line, which is not quite one thing, not quite the other, as high as I dared or as high as the ice allowed. Once again, the 'high' is an artificial imposition, derived from geometry and number, but the subliminal association with climbing, with ascent, even with some form of achievement, is inescapable. In a sense, my Arctic voyages had been modes of horizontal mountaineering, each one pushing nearer to an illusory peak; to sail to higher latitudes was also to climb higher. Here, though, one did not reach air and sky into which further ascent was impossible, but the shifting and intractable barrier of pack-ice. The peak itself was always a moving target, ultimately indefinable. Perhaps the day will come soon when a man can sail unimpeded to 90°North, thereby reaching an indisputable pinnacle. I suspect, though, that by the time that happens, the Arctic will already have lost its allure. It will no longer be the oceanic equivalent of the Alps or the Himalayas, but will have been reduced to the mundanity of the English Channel or the Mediterranean. Rousing myself from these thoughts I took myself to the hatch to survey the world, grateful that I would almost certainly be dead and gone long before that day.

21

The new morning brought with it, for the first time on this voyage, the cool crispness of a perfect Arctic day. The land away to our south – the headlands and ice caps of the Nordaustlandet – and the chunky islands strung across our starboard bow now seemed closer, more vibrant, more real. Monochrome black and white had been replaced by a palette of rich browns, greys and russets and, on the closer islands, hints of green. Everything was, for the first time, coming into proper focus.

Nordaustlandet from NW c. 20 miles

Just after breakfast a pod of common dolphins sliced around astern of us. I noted the latitude of this encounter – 80° 46'North

– as they seemed to be well beyond their normally accepted range. Perhaps it was another indication of the general move north of pelagic species as they follow the warming waters.

The sky cleared completely and with a benign Force Two breeze blowing steadily off the icecaps away to our south-east we gambolled along under six panels of the sail. *Mingming II*'s decks shone in the unaccustomed brightness and the sea turned to the deepest of indigos. Here and there a flashing silver whitecap curled gently forward. Were it not for the chill in the air and the streaks of snow and ice patterning the islands, the scene could have been equatorial as much as polar. I could scarcely believe our good fortune. For weeks we had known little but choking fog and an immutable overcast. Had I been allowed to select just one day of ideal conditions out of the whole voyage, this would have been it.

I sat in the hatchway, well-wrapped against the bite of the wind, my heart burning hot with the intensity of the moment, my alertness heightened to maximum pitch. With regular dives below to check the chart I gradually disentangled the identity of the islands spread wide across our starboard bow. Starting from the North Cape of Nordaustlandet, these were spread in a crescent from our starboard beam to almost straight ahead, and so for the moment were all more or less equidistant from us.

The first to draw my eye was Waldenøya, Walden Island, a compact protrusion of rock midway between the North Cape and the larger islands to the north and east. I wondered about the name. Had it been bestowed by some literary-minded skipper who knew his Thoreau? This seemed unlikely, but it was a pleasing thought. Subsequent research revealed an even more attractive story: the island had been named for a John Walden, who had visited the island twice with two pilots in 1773 while serving as a midshipman aboard *HMS Racehorse,* under the command of the Honourable Constantine John Phipps. Had Constantine Phipps decided to honour one of his most junior officers, probably no more than a boy, out of generosity of spirit, or with ironical humour, given that he had named one of the larger islands to the north for himself? Perhaps it was both, for I then discovered another fascinating fact: the small island further to the east, itself one of the islands that make up the Seven Islands group, was named also in 1773 for another midshipman – the then fourteen-year old Horatio Nelson. Nelson was aboard the other ship of the same expedition, the oddly named *HMS Carcass*, under the command of the even more oddly named Captain Skeffington Lutwidge.

View of the RACEHORSE and CARCASS July 31.st 1773.

Delving further, I managed to find Phipps' immediate first-hand account of the naming of Walden Island. Given that at the time, both ships of the expedition were beset by ice, some of it twelve feet thick, and were facing the serious and possibly terminal prospect of being entrapped for the winter, Phipps clearly had more important matters to deal with than mere nomenclature, as the following extract from his journal shows. It was August 1773:

5th. The probability of getting the ships out appearing every hour less, and the season being already far advanced, some speedy resolution became necessary as to the steps to be taken for the preservation of the people. As the situation of the ships prevented us from seeing the state of the ice to the Westward, by which our future proceedings must in a great measure be determined, I sent Mr Walden, one of the midshipmen, with two pilots, to an island about twelve miles off, which I have distinguished in the charts by the name of Walden's Island, to see where the open water lay.[4]

As I discover the background and write about it, I regret that I had not researched it properly before setting sail. My winter had been spent reading up on Franz Josef Land and I had given no thought to the explorational history of the Seven Islands. Had I known all this at the moment of examining them for myself, I have no doubt that my pleasure, being more informed, would have been that much keener. Those cold lumps of rock would have been warmed by the faint residue of those distant and often heroic stories. My imagination would have had more to play with. I may even have felt a modest complicity with the great Admiral himself.

I made a sketch of Walden Island in the ship's log. For some micro-meteorological reason the island was crowned

---

4   Phipps C. J. (1774). *A Voyage towards the North Pole undertaken by His Majesty's Command 1773*, J. Nourse, London, p. 63. This is yet another extraordinary book now lost to the mists of time. Not only does it recount exemplary seamanship and great bravery, but illustrates also the spirit of scientific enquiry of the time. The appendices, covering everything from natural history to astronomical observation, timekeeping, the distilling of sea water to make drinking water, meteorology and so on, along with innumerable tables showing the range of painstaking daily scientific data recorded, are longer than the main body of the narrative.

with its own halo of tight-packed and largely vertical cumulus clouds. It was an odd sight: dark rock with an overhanging wreath of symmetrical vapour. Like everything in the Arctic sky, this arrangement was short-lived; within an hour or two the clouds had dissolved away.

Waldenøya from WNW c. 16 miles

As we progressed to the north-east, Nelson Island disassociated itself from the mass of its much larger neighbour, Parry Island. Once it was in clear water, with pure blue sky for a backdrop, it revealed its extraordinary rectangular shape: sheer-sided, absolutely flat-topped, with only a few lower rocks and irregularities on its east side to spoil its symmetry. That was the impression, at any rate, from sixteen or so miles; no doubt, once closer, it would resolve into something less perfectly hewn.

My eye was now led on to the three larger and almost contiguous islands that form the heart of the Seven Islands: Parry Island, Phipps Island and, mostly obscured for the moment behind the latter, Martens Island. These were high and substantial landforms, the largest and northernmost of which, Phipps Island, was about five or six miles long on its north-south axis. They followed the typical topography of the region: a steep and vertically corrugated talus rising a good thousand or fifteen hundred feet from the shoreline to a relatively flat top. I was surprised by the general lack of snow and ice on the islands. It was there, but in niggardly well-worn streaks and patches.

Captain William Edward Parry came here in 1827 in *HMS Hecla*, to make an attempt on the North Pole. For that purpose, two flat-bottomed cutters, which Parry called sledge-boats, had been constructed for dragging across the ice. Given my lifelong addiction to the possibilities of small yachts, I cannot resist another diversion here on the nature and manning of these craft. The boats were twenty feet long and seven feet in the beam, that beam being carried well forward to give maximum capacity, in the style of the 'troop-boats' of the day. They were built at the Woolwich Dockyard, of a complex multi-skin construction designed to maintain water-tightness despite the twisting and concussion to which the boats would be subject as they were dragged across the ice. For the dragging part of their duties they were fitted with steel runners, along with horse-hair ropes and leather harnesses for the men. They were also provided with two large wheels which could be fitted forward, along with a small swivelling wheel aft for steering, somewhat like a Bath chair. The interior arrangement was no more than two thwarts and a few lockers, mainly for the navigational instruments. Each had a nineteen-foot bamboo mast and a tanned duck spritsail, giving them the look of tiny barge-boats, along with a boathook, a steering oar and fourteen paddles. Fourteen paddles? Yes, fourteen paddles, one for every member of the crew, for each twenty-foot boat had a crew of fourteen: two officers, ten seamen and two marines. So as well as being a sledge-boat, a troop-boat, a barge-boat, a Bath chair and a ship's cutter, each craft was also a kind of canoe, paddled Pacific-style, seven to a side. It was a wonderfully inventive and flexible idea.

OFF WALDEN ISLAND.

Parry and his men, one of whom we will meet again very shortly, made a valiant attempt to reach the Pole, but were thwarted by two factors. Firstly they had been misled by earlier descriptions of the ice, made by the aforementioned Captain Lutwidge in 1773, and by William Scoresby Junior in his 1820 *Account of the Arctic Regions*, which had led them to believe, erroneously, that the pack-ice hereabouts was an expanse of untrammelled smoothness. Secondly they had not reckoned with the rate of southward drift of the ice. This sometimes exceeded their daily forward progress, so that at times they were in fact going backwards, despite their superhuman efforts in atrocious conditions. They made it as far as 82° 45'North, at the time the highest latitude ever reached, before ceding and turning back. Parry estimated that in order to cover the hundred and seventy-two miles from the *Hecla*, which had been left at a safe anchorage off Low Island, well to the south-west of the Seven Islands, they actually had to traverse two hundred and ninety-two miles, of which the first hundred were over water.

Mostly hidden behind Parry Island and Phipps Island, and only to be fully revealed once we had weathered the northern point of the whole group, lay Martens Island. It was named, whether by Phipps or Parry or someone else I have yet to determine, for the celebrated German physicist and naturalist Friedrich Martens. Martens visited Spitsbergen in 1671, aboard a Hamburg whaling ship, and made a comprehensive catalogue of its wildlife, as well as conducting various experiments on its climate. His book *Voyage into Spitsbergen and Greenland* was translated into English and published in 1694 as part of an anthology of voyages under the succinct title of: *An account of several late Voyages and Discoveries to the South and North, towards the Streights of Magellan, the South Seas, the vast tracts of land beyond Hollandia Nova, etc., also towards Nova Zembla, Greenland and Spitzberg, Groynland or Engrondland, etc., by Sir John Narborough and others.*

22

In the wide bay to our south formed by the crescent of the approaching islands, fin whale spouts began to fire off. Here was Thoreau's *life pasturing freely where we never wander*. The whales kept their distance and for once I was glad of that; I could tiptoe my way around the fringes of their Arcadia without causing the least disturbance, and so maintain the division between myself as mere observer and themselves as true participants. This was, for the moment, their world, not mine. I wondered how long this final Arctic idyll could be maintained; how long it would be before the arrival of the merchant ships and container ports and oil rigs, heliports, hotels, bars, brothels, and all the paraphernalia of exploitation[5]. There was a grim inevitability about it all. The economics of perpetual growth, a perverse concept within a closed and finite system, demanded nothing less.

---

5   Three days after I passed Phipps Island a Polar bear was shot dead on the island by the crew of a cruise ship preparing for the landing of passengers.

Fin whale spout

I thought, too, about the past, and the Northern fleets which had for several centuries wreaked such havoc on the wildlife hereabouts. They had a lot to answer for, but to see those whalers and sealers as blameworthy would be to view and reinterpret history through the wrong lens. It would be too simplistic to judge them on the basis of our present-day knowledge and worldview. They too were driven by an economic imperative beyond their control, and which was largely exonerated by the potent Judeo-Christian notion that all the creatures of the world were created solely for man's benefit. Added to that was the sheer abundance of life here. The waters teemed. Maybe it seemed, for a long, long time, that the supply was endless.

There were no more than five or six whales cruising peaceably around, a mile or two to our south. Their tall spouts shimmered in the sunshine as they trailed off and dissolved into the cool air.

The wind freshened as it backed slightly towards the east. I reduced the sail to five panels and hardened the boat onto the wind as much as was compatible with keeping her moving well through the developing chop. We had lost our leading wind and were now being pushed somewhat to the north of our approaching targets: Little Table Island and Ross Island. These were now very fine on the starboard bow, two closely bound islands of complete contrast, the one tall and imposing, the other low and unassuming. My aim had been to pass close by, but that was now under threat. Just before four in the afternoon I decided to put in a board to the south-south-east in order to maintain contact with the islands. For an hour and a half we drove down towards Phipps Island, its western cliffs bright in the afternoon sun, the snow on its rounded northern highpoint all asparkle.

I would have liked to have continued longer on that board, to give maximum flexibility once we tacked again to head north-east, but a layer of cloud was approaching from the south, threatening the light. I was faced with an awkward decision: do I pass Little Table and Ross Islands closer in, but in poor light, or further off, but in better light? Keen to capture some good quality photographs, if I could, I chose the latter, and so went about to resume our approach to Western Europe's northernmost rock.

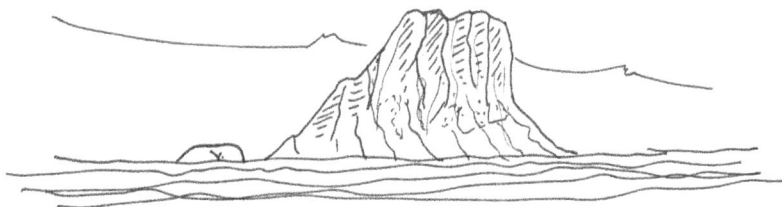

Rossøya (1.) and Vest Tavlegya (r.) from W c. 5 miles

Viewed from the west, Little Table Island puts one immediately in mind of a Gothic cathedral, a magnificent and steeply buttressed Notre-Dame, thrusting upwards to perhaps seven or eight hundred feet above the sea. Its seven or so buttresses flanked deeply riven gullies, the lower sections of which were spread with the scree and detritus forced down by ice and water. These triangular patches must have stabilised and compacted, for they were now covered with a lush carpet of green vegetation all at odds with the implacable rock above. This unexpected verdure glowed warmly under the afternoon sun, reminding me that some fifty million years ago the climate hereabouts is reckoned to have been subtropical.

To the north lay Little Table Island's squat companion, Ross Island. From any distance one would assume that the islands are conjoined, but a channel a hundred yards wide separates the two. Ross Island is flat and round, its rock bare of any vegetation apart from lichen. The first to land on it was Lieutenant James Ross, Parry's righthand man on his 1827 attempt on the North Pole. The date was the seventeenth of June. Here is Parry's own description of the naming:

> *'To the islet which lies off Little Table Island, and which is interesting as being the northernmost known land upon the globe, I have applied the name of Lieutenant Ross in the chart; for I believe no individual can have exerted himself more strenuously to rob it of that distinction.'*[6]

The then twenty-seven-year old Ross was already an experienced Arctic hand and after serving with Parry and his uncle Sir John Ross on six Arctic expeditions, went on to lead his own expeditions in the Arctic and, more importantly, the Antarctic. The naming for him of this tiny rock was only the start; eventually he had a whole sea all of his own, the ultimate accolade. Nor have we finished with Ross; he will make another unexpected appearance off the coast of Franz Josef Land.

Back on our north-easterly board we closed the islands. The sun was already slipping behind a layer of high, thin cloud, and so I was glad that I had not held on too long on

---

6   W. E. Parry, *Narrative of an Attempt to reach the North Pole… in the year 1827* (John Murray, London, 1828), p. 172.

the other tack. It was looking as if we would weather Ross Island about two miles off, close enough for good views, but still a seamanlike margin.

Our progress gradually brought all of the Seven Islands to the southward of us, transforming them from a string of separate units to one solid block, with the exception of the diminutive Nelson Island out to the west. We may as well have been looking down at a single complex headland, for all the six other islands – Ross, Little Table, Table, Phipps, Parry and Martens – were now visible and fused together with, for a little while anyway, no clear water between them.

I had imagined this moment many times over the previous few years in a hazy, unfocused way. I had, of course, no idea what to expect, but the reality still surprised me. Considering where we were, within a few miles of 81°North, everything seemed remarkably commonplace. I had not seen the least sign of sea ice, nor would I for the whole voyage; the islands were neither snow-covered nor glaciated; wind and sea were benign; navigationally it was much simpler than forcing a passage round the South Foreland or Portland Bill.

At about seven in the evening of Wednesday the twenty-fifth of July, our twenty-fourth day at sea, and in about 80° 54'North, the islands began to separate themselves out once more. A few simple transits showed we were now to the east of Ross Island. The Norwegian Sea and the Fram Strait now lay astern. For the moment we were in the Arctic Ocean, with the Queen Victoria Sea not so many miles ahead. With the wind still at east-south-east we were slanting towards the north-east and 81°North.

My plan was straightforward: for the moment we would run down our easting as close as possible to that line of latitude. It was in many ways an absurd notion, or until recently would have been considered so, but for the moment there was no reason not to. I reduced sail, though, as I needed to sleep, and had no wish to run on too far or too quickly without a good visual watch.

The Seven Islands and, to their south, the headlands and icecaps of the Nordaustlandet, fell away on our starboard quarter. The sun had gone and the light had taken on a grainy quality, although not enough to rein in the visibility. Ahead lay a great expanse of open and hopefully ice-free sea. For the moment I could relax and settle in to the next phase of the voyage. We were now, once again, way beyond the back of beyond. The chart ahead was little more than an expanse of white, crossed by no more than half a dozen transects of widely spaced soundings.

I snuggled down under my sleeping bag on the home-made cushions of my home-made bunk, pleased to have done things in my own way, on my own terms. *Mingming II* slid gently on towards an unknown sea.

23

Yes, for once I was happy to be sailing due east, and privileged too: it was unlikely that there was anywhere else along the whole circumference of the 81°North line of latitude where there was the prospect of two hundred and fifty miles of clear water. I had no concerns about the pack-ice itself, knowing that its edge now lay well to the north, perhaps ninety nautical miles or so. What I had to be wary of, though, were the breakaway agglomerations wandering about to the south of the main ice. There could well be a few of them around, bandits out hunting for septuagenarian pseudo-explorers in plastic yachts. If they could get their implacable hands on one of these, in the right conditions, they could have a field day, for there is nothing at which the ice is more adept than wrecking the ships and the dreams of those who would venture too far.

The ice has delivered many a lesson over the centuries. Foremost in my mind was the tale of the English explorer of Franz Josef Land, the fabulously rich but pathologically shy Benjamin Leigh Smith. Leigh Smith's ship the *Eira*, all one hundred and twenty-five feet and three hundred and sixty tons of her, had been built specifically for his purposes, with no expense spared, at Peterhead in north-east Scotland. Her hull was three feet thick, with her bow reinforced to a thickness of eight feet. On her second expedition to Franz Josef Land, in 1881, she was caught, in benign conditions, between the fast ice to which she was moored at Cape Flora and a sudden ingress of sea ice. She was holed in a matter of minutes, though she took several hours to settle, her topmasts still showing. Cape Flora, on the south-west coast of Northbrook Island, one of the southerly Franz Josef Land islands, was the traditional site for overwintering explorers.

As well as ice wandering down from the north, I had to bear in mind the possibility of meeting lumps of ice calving from the glaciers and ice cliffs to our south. These were unlikely to be big, and would no doubt be melting quickly, but solid ice is as hard as steel, easily capable of shattering *Mingming II*'s hull and introducing a flood of frigid water into her nice dry cabin. With her inbuilt buoyancy, *Mingming II* would probably float reasonably high and resist an immediate journey to the bottom, but an inundated yacht was an inconvenience I could do without.

My reasoning, therefore, was that if I sailed a middle course between the pack-ice and the calving glaciers, I ran the least risk of an ice encounter and an early and extremely cold bath. This did not mean, though, that my vigilance could be in any way relaxed, or that I could assume success in the enterprise, or that I should be any less ready to turn tail and make a retreat, honourable or otherwise.

In fact, as Leader of the Expedition, I knew that it would be expected of me to issue some Instructions in this regard. I therefore formulated, wrote out and delivered (to myself and the rest of the skulking crew) the following Orders:

Instructions for the Conduct of the Sailing Vessel Mingming II in waters North of 79°North Latitude and East of 20°East Longitude:

1. *Whilst under way, a regular 360° horizon check will be made, the interval of which will be determined by the following factors:*
   a) *The Ship's speed*
   b) *The level of visibility pertaining*
   c) *The weather conditions prevailing*
2. *Whilst the Crew is sleeping, sail will if necessary be reduced to limit the Ship's speed to one and a half knots.*
3. *Particular vigilance will be applied if the Ship is proceeding with the wind aft of the beam.*
4. *The Crew will ensure, through the use of the instrument provided expressly for this purpose, and at considerable expense (twenty-four pounds sterling plus postage), namely the Extra Big and Loud Timer, that periods of sleep are limited to a maximum of fifty minutes, or shorter if conditions so dictate. Between bouts of sleep full horizon checks will be made.*
5. *Should any ice be encountered in a particular area, even a single floe, then the Crew will endeavour to stop the Ship, by whatever means is appropriate given the prevailing conditions, during periods of sleep.*
6. *Should the density of floes in a given area exceed ten percent of the visible sea surface, then the Ship will be put about to sail a reciprocal course until the sea is once again clear of all ice. A new course will then be set or, if deemed necessary, a permanent retreat made.*

It was important to have a pre-ordained set of procedures, to minimise the risk of being drawn unwittingly into some kind of trap. Sea ice is notoriously unpredictable and surprisingly fast-moving, and so I had to be disciplined in my attitude towards it.

For a while, as we made our way east and my watch-keeping intensified, I seemed to see distant ice floes every time I looked out, chimera which invariably dissipated into the white-caps they only ever were. But I preferred to see ice which was not there, rather than not to see ice which in fact was there.

By breakfast-time the next morning the wind had fallen away to nothing, leaving us once more idling on a placid sea. For the moment the sun had gone too, and so we sat there in a world turned grey above and below. Way off to the south a conical mountain pushed high above the horizon, perhaps the two-thousand feet high Binneyfjellet on Prins Oscars Land, a narrow peninsula thrusting out due north from the Nordaustlandet. Other low protrusions of land showed to its east and west.

A little breeze came up from the south-west, bringing rain with it, and later that morning, as the sun tried once more to pierce the heavy cloud, an Arctic skua, the first of the voyage, passed ahead, forging north. Then a puffin and two kittiwakes passed us astern, eyes set northwards, followed by a guillemot also heading north. I wondered what was going on up there. Was I missing something? The urge to change our heading and follow the crowd was, momentarily, strong, but I resisted and held our course due east, my thoughts still fixed on the sea of the long-lived queen.

24

We had already had our fair share of heavy rain during this voyage, and the Ship's Collector of Rain was looking more and more down-in-the-mouth and, it has to be said, petulant. He had adopted the tight-lipped expression he always wore when the sail and decks were dripping with rainwater, *Why,* I could hear him demanding in that whining, offended tone he could affect just whenever it suited him, *why are we carrying gallons and gallons of water, weighing down the ship and impeding our progress, when the heavens are awash with the stuff? It is an insult to my integrity and expertise to have me idling away for hour after hour while it is pouring down outside. I could have collected enough water to last us a month in the last two hours.*

I avoided the argument. In a way, the smug, annoying fellow was right, but as the Skipper (and Leader of the Expedition) I felt more secure with all our water needs stowed away in the bilge and scattered round a dozen lockers and hidey-holes. The fact was I did not trust the Collector of Rain one inch. Despite his airs and graces, and infuriating holier-than-thou demeanour, and his propensity for blinding you with formulae and obtuse argument, I was not convinced that he could do his job as well as he professed. I suspected he was something of a charlatan, shipped aboard with certification of dubious provenance. He had only ever been put to work once, somewhere in the North Atlantic, with underwhelming results. Our water may well weigh us down and may eventually be jettisoned, but it was too important to survival to take any chances with. And anyway, all his self-important messing about with bowls and tubes and whatever paraphernalia he had secreted away for the job would upset the calm and harmony which I had worked so hard to create aboard ship.

Right at that moment I had a more important matter to consider. For a while I had been aware of an irregular but persistent graunching sound. I had first noticed it while lying on my bunk with my head close to the hull, which was somehow acting as a sounding board for the faint noise. Any sailing boat is subject to a whole symphony of tiny sounds and it took me a while to isolate this particular component and start to analyse it. Eventually I linked it to the steering system. Every time the tiller moved, there it was – a dry rubbing sound. Whatever was causing it, it did not sound too healthy. At first I thought it might be coming from a bearing in the self-steering gear, but there was something too deep-seated in the sound; I could almost feel the hull vibrating with the noise. Then I wondered about the blocks that held the steering lines. Could it be coming from one of those? Possibly, but blocks tend to squeak rather than groan. The third possibility was that the rudder shaft was rubbing somewhere within its outer tube. I had replaced the original shaft, a one-inch diameter stainless steel tube, with solid stainless steel, and I knew it was a tight fit. Moreover, by filling the lazarette with foam and sealing it, I had denied myself access to the lubrication nipple on the outer tube.

Just after lunch, then, on Thursday the twenty-sixth of July, our twenty-fifth day at sea, I exited the main hatch for just the third time of the voyage. As is my usual practice, whatever the conditions, I put on my harness and made sure I was always attached to two strongpoints. Firstly I went right aft and listened carefully to the self-steering gear. Nothing. Then I checked the steering-line blocks. No obvious sounds were coming from them, but I gave them each a squirt from the can of silicon-based lubricant I had brought out with me, for good measure. Next I examined the tiller and rudder shaft. With my hand on the top of the tiller, close to the top of the rudder stock, I could feel a vibration that matched the graunching. I sat in the cockpit and spent five minutes squirting lubricant down the top of the tube that held the rudder shaft. I disconnected the steering chain and spent some time wiggling the rudder to help the lubricant down. The graunching sound faded away. I hooked up the self-steering again and retreated to my haven below. The graunching was a mild annoyance which necessitated several more lubrications during the voyage, but it carried no structural or operational threat.

I made a quick calculation. My three exits of the hatch during the voyage so far had kept me on deck and out in the elements for about fifteen minutes in total. I had been at sea for twenty-four days, which equated to thirty-four thousand, five hundred and sixty minutes. The ratio of time spent below to time spent on deck was therefore two thousand, three hundred and three to one. Expressed differently, for every minute I had spent on deck I had spent more than thirty-eight hours below. That was the sort of ratio I liked. I did not go to sea to spend my time out in the cold and wet, crawling along bucking side-decks, wrestling with armfuls of undisciplined canvas, lurching around with the prospect of being pitched overboard at any moment. I was happy to leave all that to the more heroic type of sailor. My preference was for dryness and tranquillity, for total sail management that could be effected within a few seconds from the safety and shelter of the hatch.

This attitude, unmanly or even cowardly as it may seem, meant I always felt relaxed and in control. I could cope with virtually any weather and any circumstance with a few quick actions; I never had any fear of being overwhelmed in some way by wind and wave. Never having to go on deck, or even into the cockpit, in all but the most exceptional circumstances, in regard to the handling of the boat, I was spared any underlying dread of dangerous exposure. The exception was the launch and retrieval of the Jordan series drogue. The drogue was permanently attached to its bridle and flaked down in bins on the cockpit seats, ready for immediate deployment. However, before it could be launched, the self-steering pendulum had to be rotated out of the water and lashed upright, a manoeuvre that necessitated a few awkward minutes right at the transom. I had been through that unwelcome procedure twice on *Mingming*, but have so far been spared it on *Mingming II*.

It seems to me to be perfectly rational to organise a rig and its handling in such a way as requires the least effort and the least exposure to the elements, while still, of course, relying on no more than strong and simple mechanisms. It seems perverse to make extra work for the mere sake of it, or through lack of imagination, or through a misplaced obsession with speed. If the more easily handled rig is slightly less efficient performance-wise, it redresses the balance through a reduction of stress on its handler. The dry, relaxed and calm navigator will make better decisions than his or her exhausted and hypothermic counterpart, and perpetually good decision-making is the key to successful voyaging. The adventure, too, will be that much more enjoyable.

25

For ten years I had studied the daily ice maps of the sea in which we were now sailing. For ten years, except for an occasional relenting towards the end of the autumn, the sea here and to the east had been choked with ice: impassable, impossible, forbidden. It was a happy coincidence that the year in which I wanted to sail was also the year in which the pack-ice had receded so far. For that I was extremely grateful. If I cared to open my eyes, though, and think beyond the merely egocentric, it brought me into a confrontation with things much more timeless and fundamental. I was tempted here to write 'truths' rather than 'things', but in these days of shifting and subjective relativism, 'truth' is an elusive and dangerous concept, best left to its own devices.

The fact is that my elation at being able to run down my easting in the preposterous latitude of 81°North was tempered, deep down, so far down that had I so wished I could have completely ignored it, by a kind of sadness, a sense of loss, a strange nostalgia. It took a while to determine quite what this was and where it came from.

At first I thought it was no more than regret at the slow but accelerating death of the Arctic. It was the frozen Poles, more than any other planetary feature, which had for centuries imposed an actual and metaphorical limit on mankind's expansion. Here was a no-go area for all but the bravest or the most foolhardy. The Poles served as a constant reminder of man's ultimately puny constitution; they kept him in his place; confined him to the soft and the temperate. They also challenged him, puzzled him, infuriated him and, time after time, killed him. More importantly, they were always there, a kind of white shadow, forever haunting man's consciousness.

Now they are melting, crumbling, dissolving away, altering not simply the face of the planet, but man's relationship to it. To lose the Arctic (and perhaps in time the Antarctic too) as we have always known it will not just be a matter of a shift in geo-politics; it will be a fundamental revision of our physical and metaphorical worldview. We will lose our last true wilderness, and with it any sense of our own circumscriptions.

I felt keenly, then, that this wide-open and ice-free water at 81°North symbolised the end of an era, signalling a planetary transition whose outcomes were little thought about and certainly not fully understood. I was sailing along the cusp of a seismic shift in our species' relationship with its world.

The more I thought about it, though, and the further I distanced myself from the immediate, the more I realised that ultimately it did not matter. In the short timeframe in which we live we become overly wedded to the world as it is. To think about the Arctic purely in terms of its poetic value for a few generations of a single species was anthropocentric in the extreme. It was the kind of solipsism that ought to be avoided. This is not to forget or deny that the loss of the Arctic ice would have profound and almost inevitably terminal effects on many other species: polar bears, bowhead whales, narwhals and so on. They are unlikely to survive, but the hard fact of nature is that in the long run nothing survives.

I tried to distance myself and view the whole question in terms of geological time and the passage of millions or hundreds of millions of years. It was hard to find a reference point for such unimaginable aeons. I thought about a period of fifty million years and tried to relate it to the civilisation of man. It is now about two and half thousand years since the birth of Plato, which seemed a good starting point. How many two and a half thousand year periods would there be in the next fifty million? Twenty thousand. I thought about it another way. We are told that it is about a hundred and fifty thousand years since the emergence of early man. How many times would that period fit into fifty million years? About three hundred and thirty-three.

These mundane mental gymnastics served a purpose: they brought my perspective back into line with reality, or at least into line with a wider reality marginally less constrained by my own limited viewpoint. As much as I might lament the prospective disappearance of the Arctic, it was only ever a temporary phenomenon. In the endless cycle of global warming and cooling, whatever the stimuli, it would have disappeared anyway, only to return and disappear again, over and over, each time bringing with it a reconstituted nature. Whatever man may be doing to the planet, he is not destroying it. The planet, until the final flaring of the sun, is indestructible. What man may be destroying is his own provisional and idealised view of it. He may be destroying too, or at least curtailing, the timeframe in which he can maintain himself as a viable species. The planet itself cares nothing for that. It, and the life which clothes it, will march on regardless in a constant cycle of change and renewal.

This seemed to be a self-evident fact, and the final question I asked myself was whether it should really be cause for any sort of emotional response. Was I really justified in feeling a tinge of sadness at the juxtaposition of our own transience to the enormity of time? Wasn't it somewhat self-indulgent, too, to feel indignation at the potential disappearance of the ice, as if it had been put there solely to fuel my own sense of adventure? Ought I to be just a little less subjective about it all?

I resolved to be more accepting of the way things are. It is pointless to rail against the inevitable.

26

In an unreliable wind from the west-north-west we ran on eastwards. Sometimes mist came in, sometimes it rained, and even though on one occasion a sudden increase in wind strength set us careering along on our ear, waking me from a short sleep, the breeze was mostly on the point of fizzling out entirely. An awkward swell from the north-east robbed us of any chance of a smooth ride; the resultant pitching and rolling spilled the light wind from the sail and set the battens clattering. I gybed now and again to keep us at best possible angle to the waves, always, for the moment, sticking as close as was possible to the line of 81°North.

At six-thirty on the morning of Friday the twenty-seventh of July we reached a spot directly to the north of where we had turned round in 2014, exactly two degrees of latitude further south. We were sailing freely where four years earlier there had been solid pack-ice. Soon we would pass comfortably to the north of Kvitøya – White island –

our unattainable target of 2014. It was immensely satisfying to have thus brought what had seemed so out of reach firmly into our compass.

We were rapidly losing the warming influence of the Gulf Stream, causing a drop in temperature of both sea and air. I had not put on any warmer clothes since crossing the Arctic Circle, preferring to force my body to acclimatise, rather than pandering to its weaknesses, but I could feel that an upgrade in clothing would soon be necessary. Generally I was fine, except for my feet which, despite being now shod in moonboots and a couple of pairs of thick socks, were feeling increasingly frozen. I was soon to learn, in fact, that increased age, combined possibly with a much leaner physique, had made me more susceptible to certain aspects of cold.

I had spent some time over the previous winter trying to find out exactly where the outer limits of the Queen Victoria Sea lay. Its centre was situated indisputably to the north of the western islands of Franz Josef Land, its eastern side was delineated by the north-east curving crescent of the Franz Josef Land islands, but there seemed to be little consensus as to the position of its western border. At least one definition contradicted itself, saying that the sea lies in 81°North and 38°East, but also that it stretches as far west as the Seven Islands. Given that the Seven Islands lie in 20°East longitude, I was not sure what to make of this. I decided, for the purposes of this voyage, to make my own relatively conservative assessment of the western limit of the sea, and placed it due north of Victoria Island, in 37°East longitude. Victoria Island being part of the Franz Josef Land group, this definition kept the sea more closely linked to its original naming by Frederick Jackson, without any undue encroachment to the west and into Norwegian territory. We were closing in on this meridian: it was now just sixty nautical miles distant – a normal day's sail.

More rain came in and the wind swung round to the south-west, blowing hard and bitterly cold straight off the huge ice-cap of the Nordaustlandet. I reduced sail to a single panel as two Iceland gulls, supremely elegant and unhurried, crossed out path, heading west. I gybed yet again as the wind veered. By noon we had covered seventy-one miles and had strayed little more than three miles north of 81°North. What is more, we were now due north of Kvitøya, forty-six miles to our south. Everything was falling into place with little resistance.

My mind was now casting ahead to the north and western side of Franz Josef Land. With my compasses I drew pencil arcs from every headland, thereby showing the twelve-mile limits. I was already wondering whether my progress towards the islands was being tracked in some way. I knew that with the potential opening up of the Arctic, and the power struggles that would ensue for control of the seas, Franz Josef Land was starting to acquire a heightened geo-political status in the minds of the Russians. They were likely to be suspicious of any uninvited interloper. As is my usual practice I had not made any attempt to ask for permission to sail in Russian waters, having no wish either to confront a tortuous and thoroughly opaque Russian bureaucracy, or even to alert anyone that I may be sailing in the area. Although theoretically any vessel has right of passage through national waters, this was not something I wanted to put to the test as far as the Russians were concerned. My tactic would be always to keep at least twelve miles off the coast. In theory this would make us untouchable, but I was not so naïve as to think that I would therefore have complete protection from any form of investigation. Nor was I so naïve as to think that the Russians do not keep a good watch on what goes on in the Barents Sea and perhaps even further north, especially given that Murmansk, on the northern Russian coast, is a major hub of Russian naval operations. The Russian fleet had been greatly reduced in size since the collapse of the Soviet Union, but it was clear that the Russians maintained an extremely proprietorial attitude towards the north-east passage and any land and sea further north.

Two things possibly worked in my favour: the size of my vessel and the sheer improbability of the course I was sailing. Since its discovery by the Austrians Payer and Weyprecht, aboard the icebound *Tegetthoff,* on the thirtieth of August 1873, Franz Josef Land had invariably been approached from the south or the south-west, via the Barents Sea. No other route was possible. For all I knew I was the first navigator to make an approach from the north and west, without having entered the Barents Sea at all. There was a good possibility, therefore, that nobody would be paying much attention to the area in which I was sailing. I assumed that any surveillance would be by satellite. This did not exempt us from detection, but there was a chance we may pass unnoticed.

27

Just after midnight on the morning of Saturday the twenty-eight of July, after twenty-five and a half days at sea, we crossed 37°East longitude and so entered, unequivocally, the Queen Victoria Sea. Externally, of course, nothing changed: water and waves were just as before, the wind was as fickle and gutless, a brief spell of clear sky had ceded to thick low cloud and light rain, I was still hard at work adjusting our course and rig to keep slatting to a minimum and squeeze the best out of the light airs. Internally, I felt the elation that comes with entering new and almost forbidden territory. After four years of thought and planning, we were actually there. Once again, my relationship with the planet shifted. It was the same old ocean, doing the same old things, but my internal spacial orientations had reinvented themselves. I was seeing and feeling the world from a totally altered perspective. It seemed to me that the fact of having been nearly a month at sea, alone, and in a tiny vessel, was fundamental to the strength of this perception. The speed and unnaturalness of air travel, as a contrary example, anaesthetises us to any real sense of displacement; the globe is stripped of its scale; advanced technology makes us superhuman, but at the same time robs us of some primal elements of our humanity; our sense of the geography of where we are is somehow scrambled and enfeebled.

About a hundred and twenty miles to our east lay Ostrov Artura – Arthur Island. Halfway across that distance just one line of soundings, on a north-south axis, each sounding ten miles apart, sullied the otherwise pure white of the chart. The sea hereabouts was as virgin as it is possible to find.

An hour after entering the Queen Victoria Sea the wind swung round to the south-east. As I settled us down again under five panels of the sail I discovered that the forward end of one of the battens had chewed its way out of its restraining pocket, a result, no doubt, of the heavy slatting of the last few days. Standing in the open forehatch I made a provisional repair. I ought not to have not needed to do this. Over the winter I had strengthened all the upper batten pockets, but neglected the lower ones, on the basis that they were less prone to wear and tear, and had been fine throughout our previous voyage. My laziness was now catching up with me.

It was the middle of the night, but for once the sky had cleared completely. I could feel a tinge of warmth from the brilliant sunshine. Despite that, I was starting to feel more hungry than usual; no doubt I was burning more calories to keep warm. Later on I relented on my eating discipline and added a tin of fish to my breakfast.

Lieutenant Ross made an unexpected reappearance just before that breakfast. Having weathered his island I thought that we were done with him, but here he was again, this time in the form of the beautiful small gull first described by and named after him: the Ross's gull. It was the first I had ever seen, and so to an extent compensated for the general lack of wildlife encountered on the voyage so far. This one was an immature bird, somewhat reminiscent of a young kittiwake, but much smaller, with a short black bill. I needed to be sure that the gull really was named after the same Ross, and was pleased to unearth this extract from page 184 of Parry's *Narrative of an Attempt to Reach the North Pole, &c, in 1827*:

> *We saw, in the course of this journey, besides an ivory gull and a malle-mucke, one of the very beautiful gulls first discovered by Lieutenant Ross at Arlagnuk, in our voyage of 1823, and named, in compliment to him, Larus rossii.*

The voyage of 1823 was an attempt to find the north-west passage, and Arlagnuk is a headland in Nunavut in north central Canada. If I may be allowed one other interesting diversion, *malle-mucke* was the old Dutch whalers' word for a fulmar. It seems to have its origins in the meaning 'silly gnat', or possibly 'silly gull', a reference both to the big flocks that fulmars form, and the ease with which they could be tempted close and killed. The word has somehow shifted from the northern to the southern hemisphere, jumping species somewhere along the way: it is the origin of the antipodean term for an albatross – mollymawk. Language in any context is endlessly fascinating.

For several hours we ran on in piercing sunlight, raising, for a short while, the prospect of approaching the coast of Franz Josef Land in ideal conditions. I thought again about those Russian satellites and whether the clear sky now left us exposed to discovery. Maybe a destroyer had already been despatched to intercept this strange incursor into their private part of the Arctic.

By a strange quirk of local and planetary magnetism, the massive westerly deviation on my main steering compass, caused by its proximity to my stainless steel stove, was at that point cancelled out by the massive easterly variation in those parts – about 30° east – and so for once the compass heading actually corresponded to geographical reality. This exactitude was somewhat unnerving. I was more accustomed to going roughly one way or the other, give or take ten or twenty degrees. On the wide ocean in particular I don't get too fussed about directional precision. At any given moment there are too many variables pushing you one way or the other to allow you to delude yourself that you can actually steer a precise course. At that point I was heading more or less east, and that was good enough for me.

The wind veered to the south and fog once again rolled in. By mid-morning we were not much more than sixty miles to the north-west of Cape Mary Harmsworth, the westernmost tip of Alexandra Land. It felt dream-like, surreal, to be within a whisker of the places where so many dramas had been played out a century earlier. Frederick Jackson and a small team had endured a terrible time on Alexandra Land, caught on the icecap and unable to find a way off, it being largely edged with sheer ice-cliffs. They had criss-crossed in desperate circumstances searching for an escape route. The reading of these adventures had placed them not simply in another age, but almost on another planet, a place so remote and intangible as to only ever be the stuff of the imagination. Now that same icecap lay just over the horizon.

For a while I had been edging slightly to the north in the shifting winds, and at one point had reached 81° 17'North. This was just five hundred and twenty-three miles from the North Pole and eventually turned out to be the highest latitude we reached. For the moment, though, I had still held a more northerly objective on mind.

Our noon position put us at 81°12.4'North 41.0°East. We had covered seventy-nine miles over the previous twenty-four hours, and so were closing the islands of Franz Josef Land at a good rate. The sun tried to pierce the fog and for a while succeeded. A Brünnich's guillemot flew past, confirming our approach to land. The explorers called them 'looms', a corruption of the Dutch 'lumje', and killed them in their thousands for food.[7] Another Ross's gull appeared and flew alongside us for a moment or two, giving me the chance to photograph it.

The wind continued to veer and by now was in the south-west. This put me on alert. With the wind taking on a westerly complexion I had to be careful. Should it veer a little more and strengthen, always a possibility in this area of rapidly arising summer gales, I could quickly find myself on an awkward lee shore. Franz Josef Land is a dense archipelago, its islands criss-crossed by a web of interlocking and mainly very narrow channels, and the last thing I wanted was to be driven into that labyrinth, with its fast-moving currents, possibly ice-filled bays, and the awkward winds associated with the proximity of high icecaps. It was the stuff of nightmares, even more so as I had no permission to be there.

Unwilling to run on too blithely into a possible trap, I hardened up a little and angled in more to the south-east, towards the north coast of Alexandra Land.

---

7   This is not an exaggeration. Frederick Jackson, for example, kept a daily log of all 'game' killed. In August 1895 he records the shooting of 1,017 looms. That was just for one month out of the three years spent in Franz Josef Land. During those three years Jackson, as well as despatching a dizzying number of birds, seals and walruses, also shot 88 Polar bears: 54 he-bears, 21 she-bears, 3 unidentified adult bears and 10 cubs. The largest bear measured 8ft 2in along the back. Bear meat was the staple diet of the men and their dogs.

28

The Russians came so quickly that they were on me before I knew it. I had lain down on my bunk, well-wrapped in a blanket for warmth, for a thirty-minute nap. I was awoken by a dull throbbing sound which for a moment or two infused itself into whatever I was dreaming about before rousing me with a start. I threw off the blanket, put my glasses on, opened the after hatch and looked out. Bloody hell! A few hundred yards to windward a massive and mean-looking warship, a destroyer by the looks, was riding easily to the slight sea. A black RIB was heading our way at full tilt.

The RIB came up from astern and positioned itself just off our port quarter. There were about eight men aboard, dressed in black and heavily armed. The RIB drew slowly alongside and one of the men made an up-and-down movement of his arm, indicating that I should stop the boat. I let go the mainsheet, allowing the sail to billycock to leeward. The two craft were now side by side, rolling together uncomfortably.

The man who had signalled me to stop shouted across.

What you do here?

I am sailing.

Why you sail here? Is Russian water.

I knew full well that we were well out of Russian national waters.

International water! I shouted back.

Ha! Ha! Is very funny! You sail in Russian water! Here everything is Russian water!

Under his black beanie was a round Slavic face in the Krushchev mould, with high cheekbones and the palest of blue eyes.

I coming to arrest you!

We are eighteen miles offshore! I shouted. *You cannot arrest me!*

He laughed.

Ha! Here I do what I like!

He muttered a few words to the helmsman of the RIB, who positioned it so that the officer could grab the pushpit and swing himself aboard.

I saw red.

Jesus! Get off my boat! I screamed at him. All my Russian came flooding back. *У вас нет права! You don't have the right! Здесь международное море! This is international sea! Нет преступления плавать здесь! It is not a crime to sail here!*

The officer laughed and climbed down into the cockpit.

You speak Russian, eh? You spy. I take you to ship.

No! No! You cannot take me off! I won't leave my boat!

He unslung his Kalashnikov and pointed it at me.

You come now! Criminal English spy!

I ducked back down inside the hatch and in one practised movement closed and dogged it, locking myself into the cabin. It was no good – the butt of the Kalashnikov smashed through the glass. I grabbed the boathook from the port quarter berth and lunged it through the shattered opening, hitting the top of his thigh with the point. With his free hand the officer grabbed the shaft of the boathook, wrenched it away from me and threw it aside.

The barrel of the Kalashnikov came through the hatch. Jesus Christ. The thing was twelve inches from my head.

You very stupid man. You attack Russian officer in Russian waters. You criminal spy, Englishman. Bye bye.

He grinned a wide, toothy Slavic grin and pulled the trigger.

29

It did not happen like that, of course, but the more I played through various scenarios, should I be intercepted by the Russians, the more I realised that essentially I was defenceless. Nonetheless, I had nothing to complain about. I was there of my own free will, open to and accepting of any risks that I might be running. In any event, the greatest risk in life is an unwillingness to put oneself on the line. That way lies stifling mediocrity.

For a while, then, we ran south-east towards the coast of Alexandra Land. The weather thickened, the wind grew more muscular and so, conscious of the inhospitable ice cliffs now little more than twelve miles under our lee, I hove to under one panel. It was the typical waiting game of the awkward landfall, the application of the brakes, holding us in position until the appropriate course of action became more obvious. I was wary of those unseen islands, wary of transgressing the twelve mile limit, wary of over-confidence and complacency.

By four in the morning the wind had veered further into the west-north-west. It seemed to be easing too. Feeling that this slightly altered wind direction gave more possibility of an escape to the south should we need it, I started to head north-east, roughly parallel with the islands, and about fourteen miles off. Overhead an occasional break in the cloud raised the possibility of an improvement in the visibility, but at sea level, and especially to the east, the murk stayed resolutely thick and impenetrable. I could see nothing of the land under our lee, and never would.

The gentle ambition which I had been nurturing for several months – an attempt to reach Cape Fligely on Rudolph Island – now began to assert itself with more force. I had conceived the notion that were it at all possible, within the strictly circumscribed constraints I always put on my navigation, to reach Cape Fligely, and possibly, therefore, 82°North, it would be something worth doing. For the whole voyage I had held this thought in the back of my mind, un-obsessively. It is always as well to be flexible in one's aims. Too much single-mindedness can lead to a kind of blindness, and a blind man may not end up where he hoped.

I started to ease to the north-east, then, with the vague aim of continuing on that course as far as I felt was judicious. Cape Fligely was now about a hundred miles away and in theory quite reachable. The danger was that with the islands to our east, and the edge of the pack-ice somewhere to our north, and quite possibly not much further than 82°North, we were potentially sailing into a narrowing vector of water. That brought with if a raft of dangers. A severe storm from the south-west, and at the wrong moment, for example, could leave us comprehensively embayed between ice and land. My loose ambition was therefore tempered by a large and healthy dose of pragmatism.

There was still no ice to be seen, but the temperature inside and outside the cabin had continued to fall. My fingers and toes were permanently aching with cold. In the past I had always been relatively immune to low temperatures, but something had changed. It had begun the previous Christmas Day, in 2017. As I sometimes do, I had spent the day climbing a mountain, in this case Beinn Bhàn, near my home in Wester Ross, in snow and ice. Careless of the cold, I had spent a lot of time without gloves on. The fingers of my right hand had ended up white and numb, which I assumed would soon pass. In fact it took several weeks for my hand to return to normal. Now a similar thing was happening to both hands and both feet – a numbness interspersed with tingling and with stabbing pains. The random pain, short-lived but intense, in fingers and toes, was making sleep more difficult. I assumed that some change in my physiology, as I aged, and probably linked to less efficient blood circulation, was the cause of this new phenomenon. It was hard to understand, as hard daily work on the croft, along with many hours spent in the mountains, kept me at a high level of fitness. Perhaps I was decaying in spite of that. Time was catching up with me.

I added a thick woollen cardigan to the layers already swaddling my upper body, pulled on a second pair of heavy socks, and for the moment wore gloves most of the time. I also thought about how easy I had things compared to the explorers who had struggled around the sea-ice hereabouts. Each year they had a short window of opportunity, during the spring and early summer. During that period they had plenty of daylight, but the ice was still relatively firm and close-packed, allowing them to move around between the islands. Time and again, though, as summer advanced and the ice and snow on the floes melted, they were left in a sea of slush, often up to their thighs. Their clothes were permanently soaked in near freezing water, and became hard as boards if the temperature dropped. They ran the risk, too, of being cut off from the land and left stranded on the melting ice.

I had no cause to grumble about a little discomfort in my hands and feet.

30

We were easing along to the north-east at a comfortable distance from the coast and closing the distance to Cape Fligely. At midday on Sunday the twenty-ninth of July, our twenty-eighth day at sea, I took our position: 81° 15.3'North 46° 26.2'East. This put us about nineteen miles to the west-north-west of Arthur Island. I paged through my handheld GPS and was startled to see our speed over the ground – close to seven knots. I assumed this must be a temporary aberration, but a few minutes of observation confirmed the fact – we were being swept to the north-east at a rate well beyond our speed through the water. Whatever it was that was helping us along, be it tide or current or both, was running at close to three knots. There was of course no way to unpick what was causing this. The chart was devoid of soundings, let alone data on tides or currents. I doubt that even the Russians have tide tables for Franz Josef Land. There was a logic to the idea of a strong north-easterly current here. The North Atlantic

Current curls round the top of Svalbard, then may well continue east until it hits the barrier of the Franz Josef Land Islands, which divert it more to the north.

My reaction to this was pretty much instantaneous. If we were becalmed, we ran the risk of being carried to the north-east, towards that narrowing vector between ice and land, at anything up to sixty or seventy miles a day. We could conceivably be carried into the pack-ice within thirty or forty hours. Conversely, if we had heavy weather from the south-west, the trap would be doubly difficult to escape if we had to contend with a strong adverse current as well as a headwind. Both of these scenarios were unthinkable propositions; both of them a risk too far. The only prudent course of action was to go about and head south-west, as soon as possible.

This rapid and unexpected change of orientation was quickly absorbed; over the years I have become accustomed to bending to circumstance without regret or resistance. The outward leg of the voyage was over and that was that. It was not in any way premature. We had simply reached the limit of rational endeavour, a limit which bore no relationship to time or place.

I went about, then, and settled the boat on a course to the south-west, sailing full and bye in a freshening west-north-westerly. I was still acutely conscious of the unseen islands under our lee and so pressed on hard, knowing I would not breathe easily until we had weathered Cape Mary Harmsworth and created proper sea-room on all sides. I wanted to maintain, if possible, a minimum twelve-mile offing as we passed the Cape, thus retaining a kind of navigational and geo-political purity. Put differently, I had no wish to mess with ice-cliffs or Russians, and so would keep my distance.

The breeze blew up harder and backed slightly, forcing us hard on the wind. I opened the after hatch to re-tension a steering line and a massive bull walrus heaved out of the water thirty feet astern. He was a giant, much bigger than any of his cousins whom I had met to the north of Hopen four years previously. He gave me a startled and extravagantly toothy look, what with his yellow fangs each a good two feet long, and rolled forward under the water, showing off, as he did so, a back as brown, broad and bulky as a Chesterfield sofa.

Walrus

For a week or two I had been experiencing some pain, on and off, in the big toe of my right foot. I had ignored it, but it had become particularly insistent and so, in a moment of weakness, I asked the Ship's Doctor *and* Dentist to take a look at it. The insufferable and chronically underworked fellow was of course delighted at having the opportunity to show off his expertise. I peeled off the two layers of thick socks and exposed my foot. It was not a wholesome sight: an old man's pediment that had not seen the light of day, nor, it must be said, a bar of soap, for some considerable time. The nail of my big toe, pulverised by untold miles of hillwalking, looked particularly unappealing: a cloudy and pock-marked whitish-yellow slab that bore no relationship to the flaking flesh around it. I distinctly heard the good doctor draw a breath of disgust. Nonetheless, true to his Hippocratic oath, he carried on ministering, prodding delicately here and there as if examining the facial pustule of a leper.

Does that hurt?

A bit

Hmmm.

The doctor said nothing for a while.

Well then? I asked.

Hmmm. Yes, yes. Interesting. Most interesting. Yes. Yes. Yes.

What do you think, then?

Well, most definitely a contusion of the incremental malavoid febricum. Most definitely. Or something along those lines.

Silence.

And?

And what?

What do we do about it?

The Ship's Doctor *and* Dentist thought for a moment.

There are two options. The first is amputation. But I wouldn't advise that. Bit out of practice.

Silence.

And the second option?

Hmmm. Well. Aspirin I think. One…or maybe two. Twice a day. Or perhaps three times. Or four. Should do the trick.

I thought about it.

There is just one problem, Doctor.

That being?

We don't have any aspirin.

Ah well. Not my department, old boy. I'm a diagnostician, Sir, and if I may say so, one of the best around. Been telling you for years to appoint a Ship's Dispenser of Pills.

Well, anyway, thank you. That has been extremely helpful.

The Ship's Doctor *and* Dentist suddenly looked uncommonly pleased with himself. I well knew that self-satisfied face.

Well, you know, medical training and all that. Can't expect the layman to understand these things. Anyway, get dressed and run along now. Let me know if you would like a follow-up consultation.

I repacked my foot into its various coverings, glad to get it out of sight. It was still hard to believe that this execrescence at the end of my leg was part of the same organism as myself. I pulled on my moonboot to complete its immurement and willed myself to forget about the damn thing. That is the best cure for most ills.

31

The wind backed into the west and freshened. I hardened up and drove on to windward, keen to weather Cape Mary Harmsworth with a good margin and on a single board. Should the wind back further we faced the prospect of an awkward slog to clear the land and find open water. My calculations showed that should we drift too far to leeward we would cross the twelve-mile limit into Russian waters. I wanted to avoid this if at all possible, and so pushed on much harder than is my normal habit. With two panels set we forced our way through the steep head seas, rearing and pounding as we went, shovelling great lumps of green water over the bow and into the forward windows of the observation pod. It was exhilarating, yes, and *Mingming II*, so stiff and sturdy, hurled herself into the challenge without a quiver, but with fifteen hundred miles or more of sailing still ahead of us I would have preferred our progress to be a little more sedate.

The weather had closed in once more and I knew that there was now little prospect of any sight of Franz Josef Land. Well, so be it. I was not prepared to risk going in closer, nor was there any sense in holding position in the hope that the murk might lift at some point. There was no choice but to keep going and to accept the vagaries of fortune.

It was by now blowing a good Force 6 but I held on to our sail, unwilling to allow any let-up in our windward speed. I noticed that it was on this same day, July the twenty-ninth, that we had reached 79°North, just to the east of Abeløya in Kong Karls Land, in 2014. On both of *Mingming II's* voyages, then, we had arrived at the outward extremity on exactly the same date. It was one of those meaningless coincidences that can easily be invested with more significance than they merit.

All that day and all the following night we powered on into the head sea. I tracked our progress carefully on the chart, keen to record the moment when we were to the west of Cape Mary Harmsworth and therefore clear of any potential trap.

It was hereabouts that in July 1895 Frederick Jackson and five of his men came close to disaster. They had set out from their camp at Cape Flora on Northbrook Island to explore to the west, forcing their way through the ice in a twenty-five foot whaler named *Mary Harmsworth*, after the wife of the expedition's sponsor. On July the twenty-second, Jackson wrote:[8]

> *We also discovered a cape to the west of Cape Lofley, which I named Cape Mary Harmsworth (bearing 306°) after Mrs. Harmsworth and our boat. This cape is beyond the land seen by Mr Leigh Smith. Both it and Capes Ludlow and Lofley appear from here to be without beaches or vegetation, and to be nearly overrun by the glacier behind them.*

---

8   *A Thousand Days in the Arctic, Volume 1*, Frederick G. Jackson, Harper and Brothers 1899, p.339ff.

Having waited on the shore of George Land for several days while the whale boat went to fetch extra supplies, they set out on July the twenty-eighth to try to round Cape Lofley and the newly discovered Cape Mary Harmsworth, ten miles or so to the north-west:

We had gone through much ice, and as we sailed on towards Cape Lofley it became much closer, and our progress, owing to it and the wind freshening and the whole coast being glacier-faced, rendering landing impossible and offering no shelter, more and more risky. At 9pm we rounded Cape Lofley and ran on to within five or six miles of the cape to the west of it (Cape Mary Harmsworth)...The wind had now increased to nearly a moderate gale, and the ice had become very close... We had taken in a reef in the lug sail, and had now continually to put the boat's head up into the wind and to shake the sail to avoid gusts.

With the wind still freshening and with the prospect of being smashed against ice floes, they turned back, but matters deteriorated further:

At 10.30 pm the wind increased to a fresh gale and occasionally to a strong gale in the gusts...Things now began to look very nasty. We could proceed under sail no longer, and there was literally nothing for it but to try and weather it out in the open. We made a deep-sea anchor with three oars, to which we lashed the ice-anchor, and with about twenty fathoms of line attached to it from the bows brought the boat's head round to the sea. The sea rapidly increased and huge breakers threatened to swallow us up at every moment. They rose like mountains above our heads, and each one seemed about to engulf us.

Chilled by seawater, sleet and snow, and with little to eat except biscuits and two raw 'dovekies', the Arctic explorers' name for black guillemots, they were driven further offshore by the north to north-east gale. By the time they were forty miles off, after almost three days, they thought they had no chance of survival. Fortunately for them the gale went round to the west, and during a temporary lull they managed to claw their way back to the land. Even getting ashore was difficult:

After about six hours' sailing, fairly racing through the water at five to six knots an hour, so that collisions with ice were a serious danger, necessitating my keeping a man in the bows as look-out, we reached the land, which on nearer approach proved to be Cape Grant; and we ran round to the north-east side, hoping to find it sufficiently protected by the headland to enable us to land without damaging our boat or drowning ourselves. She, however, got nearly swamped, and loose ice came thumping in upon her with the sea and stove a plank as we ran for the narrow beach. Owing to their weakened condition, Armitage, the doctor and Child all got duckings in getting ashore; but this, I think, made little difference, for we were all as wet as we could be already. We at last got everything out of the boat, and hauled her up to the very narrow beach. We were all of us more or less weak, and we had considerable trouble in doing this.

They had managed to get ashore on the thirtieth of July, before the gale once more blew up hard from the west. Just after midnight on the morning of another thirtieth of July, a hundred and twenty-four years later, we passed to the west of Cape Mary Harmsworth, just eighteen miles off. The cape was unseen, and the memory of the crew of the *Mary Harmsworth* all but gone, their past endeavours no more than distant ghosts dancing on a cold and forgotten sea.

32

The Russians came so quickly that they were on me before I knew it. I had lain down on my bunk, well-wrapped in a blanket for warmth, for a thirty-minute nap. I was awoken by a dull throbbing sound which for a moment or two infused itself into whatever I was dreaming about before rousing me with a start. I threw off the blanket, put my glasses on, opened the after hatch and looked out. Bloody hell! A few hundred yards to windward a massive and mean-looking warship, a destroyer by the looks, was riding easily to the slight sea. A black RIB was heading our way at full tilt.

The RIB came up from astern and positioned itself just off our port quarter. There were about eight men aboard, dressed in black and heavily armed. The RIB drew slowly alongside and one of the men made an up-and-down movement of his arm, indicating that I should stop the boat. I let go the mainsheet, allowing the sail to billycock to leeward. The two craft were now side by side, rolling together uncomfortably.

Standing in the bow of the RIB was a man dressed, like the rest, in black combat gear, but with an inordinate amount of gold leaf on his epaulettes. As the RIB neared he waved, and shouted:

Hello! Hello! Welcome to Franz Josef Land!

I waved back. *Thank you!*

The man in the bow, fifty-something, lean and authoritative, was smiling broadly.

You are Roger, I think! he shouted.

Yes, how did you know?

Would you do me the honour of inviting me aboard your ship? Then I can tell you.

He spoke English easily, with just a slight Russian accent.

Yes, of course. Welcome aboard!

He grabbed the pushpit and climbed smoothly over into the cockpit, careful to avoid the cat's cradle of control lines as he went.

Please, come below, I said.

Once he was down the hatchway I put the cushion onto the wide lower companionway step.

Please. Sit down.

I sat further forward, opposite the chart table. With two people aboard, the cabin suddenly seemed tiny. My visitor ran his eyes around the bunks, lockers, compasses, shelves and over-laden hooks. Then he stuck out his hand.

Pleased to meet you, sir. I am Captain Yuri Lermontov.

Captain? You are the captain of that destroyer?

Yes, I am captain. She is my ship, just like this Mingming is your ship. But, you know, I would like your ship just as well.

'But how did you know my name, and the yacht's name?'

He laughed.

Ha! We have been tracking you, you know. There was a clear day a couple of days ago and our satellites took photographs. They were sent to me. Nobody was worried about you. Ha! You are going one way then another, wandering about as slow as a snail. Not a military threat, I think. But I looked at the photographs. They are very good, our satellites, they show everything. And I recognised your ship! I said – Oh! That is Mingming!

You know Mingming?

Of course. I have read your books, in Russian and in English. I love ocean sailing. I am so pleased to be aboard and to meet you.

I was stunned. He carried on:

You know Mikhail Soldatov, I think.

Mikhail Soldatov? Of course. We sailed together in the Jester Challenge. I took his lines when he arrived at Plymouth. And we met again at the Moscow Boat Show.

When I was junior officer he was my commanding officer. We would sometimes sail together. Unfortunately I cannot stay long. I asked permission from my superiors just to check you out, to be sure you were not a threat. Of course I only wanted excuse to come aboard. Thank you for inviting me.

You are welcome, I said. *It's a great pleasure.*

He stood up and climbed back out of the hatch. The RIB came alongside. Captain Lermontov said something and one of his men handed him a large plastic bag. The Captain leaned down the hatchway.

This is for you. A bottle of vodka, some Russian black bread baked this morning, some cheese and Russian pickles. I remembered you don't eat meat. Ha! When you had to eat Jimmy's sausages! Very funny! So no meat. Only caviar! Goodbye and good luck!

He transferred back to the RIB, which sped off, sending up a high plume of white water.

33

It did not happen like that, of course. The Russians never came, ever. I touched briefly on the edge of their territory and was soon gone, unseen and ignored.

The wind eased a little and thick fog swirled in. I drank some lime juice cordial and studied the chart. We were heading south-west, still hard on the wind, with the prospect of passing to the east of the most westerly of the Franz Josef Land islands, Victoria Island. I would have liked to have sailed down to the west of Victoria Island, thereby cutting through the twenty-four-mile passage between it and Kvitøya, but that would have entailed a long beat to windward. All I could do was hold my course and see if any opportunity arose to approach either of the islands a little closer.

Sunshine tried to pierce the fog. The wind eased further. The fog thinned a little, but there was no escaping the cloying humidity which kept the horizon always indistinct, bathed as it was in a thick and persistent veil of moisture.

At six that evening Victoria Island lay thirty miles to our west. We were passing out of the Queen Victoria Sea and into the Barents Sea. I derived a moment of childish pleasure at the thought of approaching the Barents Sea from the north, and wondered whether I would ever grow up, or whether I would ever want to.

I had been waiting for a while for calmer conditions, as there were a couple of repairs that needed doing. A batten parrel – the line that holds a batten to the mast – had managed to unlash itself and required re-tying. An aft batten pocket needed attention too: a batten was starting to work its way out. I stood up in the forehatch and re-lashed the batten parrel, grateful that I could effect repairs at the mast without ever having to go on deck. While I was at it I re-tensioned a few more of the parrels; after twenty-eight days of hard use they had stretched and slackened a little. Transferring aft to the main hatch, I then put an extra lashing on the errant batten end and its pocket, a repair that served for the rest of the voyage.

Just after nine that evening we crossed 80°North. We had spent eight days north of that heady latitude, much of that time above 81°North. There was no question that my sense of the world and its geography had been recalibrated during that time. I had grown accustomed to being there and looking downwards, as it were, on the distant world as we know it. The unattainable had achieved a kind of normality. I would never think of the High Arctic in the same way as before. It may well be that within a few years there will be nothing out of the ordinary in sailing well above 80°North, but for the moment it still seemed magical to have inserted myself so unequivocally into that implausible wilderness.

We carried on to the south-west for a while, and I thought that any chance of seeing either Victoria Island, or its Norwegian neighbour Kvitøya, White Island, was gone for good. Four years earlier ice had kept me from them; now it was an adverse wind and poor visibility. Banks of fog were still tumbling in at regular intervals, robbing the narrow world around us of any form or depth. The wind started to back, forcing our course more directly towards the south and an empty sea bounded, several hundred miles away, by the north coast of Russia. I had no desire to sail on into these nondescript waters; if possible I wanted to keep some kind of contact with the islands of eastern Svalbard. The wind backed a little further and so in the early morning of the thirty-first of July I went about to head west-north-west, a course that would bring us back up towards Kvitøya, passing close to the south of Victoria Island as we went.

For almost a whole day we worked our way towards Kvitøya in a fading wind. Flocks of kittiwakes overtook us, heading purposefully the same way. Our presence piqued their curiosity; anything on which a kittiwake can land will draw them in. Eleven Arctic terns flew west in chattering companionability. The occasional puffin and Brünnich's guillemot passed by too, cutting through the inflexible grey that seemed to hold us captive. By mid-afternoon we were ten miles due south of Victoria Island. I kept a constant vigil in the hatchway, examining every evolution of the mist and cloud to our north, straining with eyes and binoculars to decipher anything that might be classed as land, but without success. The fog lifted a little; a streak of hazy blue sky appeared for a while low over the northern horizon; I allowed myself just a little optimism; once or twice I momentarily convinced myself that a darker shadow was *terra firma* rather than thicker murk, but was always eventually forced to concede my error. The fog dissolved away, but in its place came a thick layer of cloud so low that it seemed to graze the masthead. This heavy stratum comprehensively obscured the sun and filtered away the light, darkening the world and leaving the moisture-heavy air almost as impenetrable as the fog which had gone before.

It was hopeless. The wind was fading and, it seemed, nothing would ever show itself. I thought about the all the efforts I had made, over the course of three long voyages, to get to this very spot. I might easily have convinced myself that I *deserved* some better luck; that I had *earned* it. I might easily have convinced myself that it was *not fair*. I might have done, but I kept that sort of irrationality at bay. I *deserved* nothing. *Fairness* is a concept without traction in the natural world; and I had already *earned* rewards far beyond my due during the three voyages I had made to Svalbard and thereabouts. I stared at the impenetrable horizon and cleared my mind of any sense of entitlement and, by extension, the expectation that goes with it.

A small but growing patch of brighter sky ahead of us intruded into the general gloom. I assumed for a while that there must be a minute break in the cloud cover, but there was something odd about the light; the underside of the clouds glowed with a piercing whiteness. At ten that evening, as we idled gently along under six panels of the sail, I suddenly realised what I was looking at: iceblink. I had seen this phenomenon once or twice before, but never on this scale or with such intensity. Light was reflecting off the ice below, back up to the sky, and illuminating the cloud above. I pulled out my binoculars and studied the horizon more closely. There it was, directly under the widening patch of glowing cloud – the broad and gently arching whaleback of the Kvitøya icecap. The top of the glacier was marked by a thin line of salmon pink light, a narrow neon strip that delineated the icecap's perfect curvature; below that, the ice was of a grey virtually indistinguishable from that of the cloud above us. The iceblink was centred above the highest point of the glacier, its heart as deeply white and glowing as molten iron. Kvitøya is a sizeable island, nearly twenty-five miles long on its west-east axis, and as we moved closer the extremities of the glacier stretched right across the horizon.

Ice Glace over Kvitøya . N 80° 5' E 35°

It was a moment of great relief to have finally brought this elusive island into view. In making our board back to the north-west we had crossed 80°North once again, and so had made up the degree of latitude that had escaped us four years earlier. Our position at eleven that evening – 80° 6' North 35° East – had virtually marked the edge of the pack-ice in 2014. The wind eased and we rolled softly in a sea devoid of any sign of ice.

I decided to put about and head south once more. Within a few minutes the iceblink faded and Kvitøya was largely lost behind a veil of murk that robbed the glacier of its definition. Within an hour or so of changing course we were becalmed. I exited the hatch for only the fourth time in thirty days, in order to adjust the span between the top two battens, which was showing signs of chafe. The span is the line joining the aft end of the battens, which runs through a block attached to the multipart mainsheet. Hard use was chafing the line and so I adjusted it to give the most worn part less exposure to potential damage. As I worked I could hear the Kvitøya glacier rumbling.

We lay there for twelve hours in a glassy calm. Light rain peppered us from time to time. Fog eddied through. Two kittiwakes shared the foredeck. I breakfasted early, drank a mug of hot bouillon and retired to my sleeping bag for a brief sleep. At nine in the morning two harp seals came in to examine us. The sky to the south-west brightened a little.

34

We lay there waiting for a wind, as so many hundreds of times before; a wind that would bring us down to the south-west and once more to Abeløya, our turning point four years earlier.

It is easy to impose order and purpose retrospectively; to winkle out precise motives where in fact there were none; to attribute grand design to essential chaos. And so I must be careful not to give a false impression that everything was precisely planned to turn out the way it did. I could easily fool myself on this, and induce myself to believe that there was more purpose and prescience to my voyages than was the case. As I sit now at my writing desk and survey the gently rippling loch and the high crags, and as I think about these last three outings to the High Arctic, I can see clearly that there was a geometry and an inevitability about each voyage's contribution to the final ensemble. I cannot swear, however, that I saw it that way from the outset, that the final neatness of it all resulted from a conscious act of will. Nonetheless, I know, and can be sure, that neither was it all random. Somewhere deep in my psyche I was working, slowly but with a sure hand, towards the expression of the limit of my possibility: my final voyage.

Mingming's voyage to 80°North, to the north-west of Spitsbergen, was the first reconnaissance of the truly high latitudes. I needed to know. Could I sail a twenty-foot slip of a boat there and back? What would it *feel* like? Was the boat adequate for the job, and perhaps for greater demands? Was the fundamental idea of singlehanding a tiny, engineless craft to the northern limits of the ocean truly viable or not? That voyage gave the answers to so many questions and resulted in the creation of *Mingming II*. I knew, as a result of that voyage, that everything was viable, but that I needed a slightly different ship – longer on the waterline and well-canvassed for light airs. Fleetness of foot and handiness in the fickle summer winds of the Arctic High were essential; that much I had learned.

Mingming II's maiden voyage, to 79°North and the spot we were now approaching once again, tested a different set of questions. It was one thing to make a voyage in the relatively benign climate of the North Atlantic, sailing in the warm waters of the Gulf Stream, but what of the Barents Sea? As you go north there you meet ice sooner, for there is no warming influence. And what would it *feel* like to be *there*, in the wilder, more remote and less hospitable waters east of Svalbard? How far north could a man sail there and not feel that he was indulging in no more than stupidity? Well, I went, and I did not feel unduly stupid.

I had by then caught Svalbard in a pincer movement – 80°North to the north-west and 79°North to the east. That had provided a great deal of satisfaction, but the geometry was incomplete. Although each voyage had its own pleasing shape, as they had both encompassed legs out to the west to take in Jan Mayen, once on the outward leg, once on the return, I was left essentially with two sets of coordinates linked to my home port of Whitehills: two straight lines. Those two straight lines lacked form, body, shape. They had limited meaning, and ultimately left me dissatisfied.

It was not merely, then, the simplistic desire to achieve an ever-higher latitude which was the driving force behind so much effort. There was also a hankering in there that was deeper and more elusive: the need to find a voyage of the most satisfying shape and form; the need to trace an imaginative trajectory across the face of the ocean and to mark, in a way, a path that was strictly my own. Was it far-fetched to view the seas in which we had been sailing as a clean canvas now ready for inscribing? *Mingming II's* wake had drawn what was perhaps the first line of its kind across hitherto impossible waters. For a few brief days I had taken ownership of that part of the planet; made it my own. It hardly constituted a great achievement, or a life's work. Maybe there was no meaning there beyond the fulfilment of a tenuous and intensely personal imperative; and maybe that imperative was itself no more than an illusion, or more properly a self-delusion. Unless we are saints or nihilists we all have to find something to want, something to drag us along from day to day. One man collects beer mats; another practises the trombone; a third sails in distant seas. Maybe none of it is anything but displacement activity, a pretence at purpose, a false idol that distracts from the essential absurdity of petty existence.

I was wary, then, of attributing too much significance to the venture or to my conscious role in it. I was doing what I was impelled to do, but the source of that impulsion was still a complete mystery. It was both inaccurate and illogical to allow myself any meaningful credit for what I was up to; I was being driven along like spray in the wind, as I had been for the whole of a long and convoluted lifetime.

35

The calm persisted. I made two attempts to get under way again as patches of moving air darkened the water with a brief patterning of catspaws, but both attempts yielded nothing but wasted effort and cold hands. At eleven that morning we got going more definitively in a light breeze from the east-south-east. Our noon position put us a little under two miles to the north of 80°. Just after one o'clock there was a great commotion around the boat as an Arctic skua harried a kittiwake round and round, up and down, both the birds twisting and turning with lightning-quick reactions. The skua finally disengaged, its efforts unrewarded. The breeze petered out once more and I dropped the sail. The weather thickened and the low curve of Kvitøya was lost forever in the pall of heavy air astern.

At three a wind came in again from the east-south-east and this time it was the real thing, soon forcing us down to four panels as we plunged south-west. I hardened up to make sure we would have a good clearance to the windward of Abeløya, which by midnight lay about forty-five miles ahead. It was as well that my natural caution induced me to claw up to windward, as the wind soon began to veer towards the south, narrowing the vector through which we could clear Abeløya's circle of low rock.

For fifteen hours we sped south-west, sometimes under just three panels, sometimes under four, in what was now a stiff breeze. Another marauding drama was enacted around the boat as two long-tailed skuas attacked a whole group of kittiwakes. Once again the battle petered out unresolved. I was glad of the entertainment though, for we were oppressed by thick and unrelenting grey from all sides, suffocated by the solid mass of cloud bearing down from above, blinded by the constant swathes of fog. Any relief from the formlessness and monotony of this encircling pall was welcome.

I kept a tight track on our progress, marking a regular position on the chart as we closed the eastern end of the Kong Karls Land islands. Abeløya itself is scarcely more than a rocky reef, and therefore not to be trifled with, and the southern bay of the principal island, Kongsøya, is peppered with outlying rocks and small islands. The area we were approaching is hazardous enough in clear conditions, doubly so in fog.

On we plunged, and a kittiwake put on another show as it tried to catch the long fabric tail of the wind vane in its beak. It came in several times, positioning itself with superb aeronautical control and jabbing at the snaking, snapping strip of spinnaker cloth. What the attraction was, or what the kittiwake hoped to achieve, I have no idea. I have noticed that once kittiwakes get an objective in mind, they can persist against all rational evaluation of their chances of success. This one did succeed in managing to take the end of the tail in its beak, a considerable achievement which served no purpose whatsoever. It let go, and after playing around a little longer, glided off into the fog.

At six in the evening of Thursday the second of August, our thirty-second day at sea, we crossed 79°North at a point just six miles east of Abeløya, within about four miles of our 2014 position, and thereby connected the turning points of my two previous voyages. It was immensely satisfying to have thus brought order and reason to what had commenced as random explorations. The moment also marked our exit from unknown territory; from here on we were back on more familiar ground. My intention from this point was, winds allowing, to more or less follow our 2014 route, revisiting the east Svalbard islands: Edgeøya, Hopen and Björnøya. I had no especial wish this time, though, to then make a wide arc out to the west to take in Jan Mayen. I did not rule that option out entirely, if it were forced on us by adverse winds, but my preference this time was to head back to the Moray Firth as directly as possible.

Abeløya, although so close, lay hidden in the murk, as did Kongsøya, now just eight miles to our north-west. There was a subtle difference, though, between the invisibility of these islands and that of the unseen islands of Franz Josef Land. As far as the latter were concerned, I could only imagine what lay behind the fog, but having previously spent several days around the Kong Karls Land islands in sometimes perfect conditions, I knew exactly what it was that I could not see. The essence of the islands – their heights, contours, glaciers, size, character and so on – was firmly imprinted on my memory, and so I could see them in my mind's eye almost as clearly as if they had been truly visible. Nonetheless, I would have liked to have seen the islands in the flesh, as it were, as much as anything just to check *that they were still there.* The empiricist in me preferred proof to supposition, external sensory perception to the mere exercise of the imagination.

It was all very well for me to convince myself that I knew exactly what it was that I could not see, but how could I be sure? As far as Kongsøya was concerned there was, if my chart was correct as regards an abundance of small islands and rocks to its south, no safe way of coming in closer to verify its continued existence. Svenskøya, though, the south-westerly island of the group, towards whose eastern end we were now heading, was a different matter. There were no outlying hazards on our line of approach. I decided that if the poor visibility continued, denying proof of the proximity of land, I would sail in close to Svenskøya and satisfy myself that I was not giving way to delusional thinking. The thought occurred to me that were I still a younger man, I would probably still have had confidence in my internal convictions. Age has taught me to check, check, and check again. Increasing knowledge brings with it an awareness of the fragility of that knowledge; the more you know, the less you know you know. I had learned, too, to be surprised at nothing. Had the fog cleared and revealed an unblemished horizon, with not a lump of rock or ice in sight, I would not have been unduly astonished.

36

I had fond memories of Svenskøya – Swedish Island. It was the first of the Kong Karls Land islands which we had raised in 2014. We had lain some miles off the island, to its south-east, in a magical misty calm. On that day the thin and shifting fog was confined solely to sea level, and higher up the sky was clear, so that there was always a play of sunlight through the dense droplets of moisture which hung about us, creating mirages and shifting rainbows. Now and again the distant cliffs of Kongsøya – King's Island – had shown themselves momentarily where the mist had thinned.

This time there was no sunshine, no magic, no delicacy in the play of light; everything was oppressive and sombre. I eased *Mingming II* off the wind slightly, to head due west towards the broad and high south-eastern face of the island. Capes five miles or so apart stand at each end of this face: Cape Weissenfels at the north-east end, and Cape Hammerfest at its south-west end. The navigator must be careful here, for low projections of rock snake out from both capes on the same axis as the main talus, thereby elongating the hazard, and making any close passing of either cape impossible.

I kept a constant watch into the mist. Occasional bands of common terns bounced past, squeaking jauntily to each other as they went. The wind eased slightly and I increased the sail to five panels.

Just before noon a darker shadow began to assert itself into the murk ahead of us, confirming that all was well with the world; everything was still where it should be. Shadow became form; form became rock; rock became a lofty and corrugated cliff-face topped with a few niggardly patches of ice. On our starboard bow Cape Weissenfels (its name, perhaps inadvertently, suggesting something along the lines of 'white mountain') dropped gently towards its projecting reef and the sea beyond; on our port bow Cape Hammerfest was more vertical in form, angular and more truly cape-like.

These cliffs did nothing to lift the day's impression of unmitigated dreariness. Robbed of light, sparkle, colour, the rock remained stolidly dour and grim-faced. There have been many times when the silence of a remote and unpeopled Arctic island has somehow evoked in me a sense of geological time and its almost inconceivable temporal scale; but at this moment, on this day, the silence was not simply mute, but totally uncommunicative. I stared at the island and saw nothing but vacant drabness and desolation.

We were by then just three miles off, and so I hardened up, back onto the wind again, to make sure we cleared the south-western reef with plenty to spare. As we edged to the south-west once more and passed Cape Hammerfest, the western side of the island, twenty miles or so of talus clothed in a mantle of dying glaciers, came into view. That long line of black rock offset by dull-white ice only enhanced the hopelessness of the scene. There was nothing there to redeem the pervading sense of futility; even the stubbornness of matter seemed pointless and perverse. This emptiness was, it must be said, no more than a fleeting feeling of the moment. Flat light and monochrome had undermined the nobility of nature.

Svenskøya from SW c. 6 miles

I raised another panel of the sail, giving us the whole, fully turbocharged shebang, and we skipped fluidly along towards the south-west, across the Olgastretet – the Olga Strait, heading, as we had four years earlier, for the north-west shoulder of Edgeøya. Inevitably, I thought again about Olga – *beautiful dorter of rich Russian oligarch* – whose presence I could never quite shake off. She had sent me a message in a bottle which I had almost picked up in the Greenland Sea. She had even managed to telephone me. She was clearly a very sweet and resourceful girl, if a tad demanding, like most daughters of the super-rich. I hoped that she had not taken my rejection of her too badly. If I ever got the chance, I would do my best to explain to her that I had nothing against her personally, but that it can become tiresome to be forever chased by rich and beautiful women.

The wind strengthened once more, and by the end of the afternoon we were down to four panels. Svenskøya was long since lost astern. The Olgastretet is about fifty miles wide, and so I had plenty of time to think about navigational tactics once we neared the land on its western side. With the wind in the south-east and showing signs of backing towards the east, I had to be careful, as we were approaching a lee shore. I knew that shore well, having sailed down the ice cliffs of Edgeøya four years earlier. In bright sunshine with a fair wind it was a magnificent place to be, but the prospect now was of fog and a foul wind. Circumspection was called for.

The cloud overhead was so thick that we seemed to be living in a permanent twilight, and this had an unforeseen practical consequence: at eleven that evening the red light on the regulator of my solar panel came on, replacing the green light which had shown steadily for the thirty-three days of the voyage so far. Despite the fact that there had been no drain on the battery, apart from the green light of the regulator, and despite the fact that for several weeks we had been in twenty-four-hour daylight, the battery voltage had dropped below the level the regulator deemed acceptable. This had happened to me once before, during *Mingming's* voyage to the Davis Strait, and I knew that unless we had days of brilliant sunshine, the battery was unlikely to recharge to its proper level. I had replaced the old battery with a brand new one prior to leaving. Perhaps the solar panel was losing its efficiency. The battery is only used for powering my navigation lights, so for the moment there was no problem, as they would not be needed for a while. The difficulty would come as we neared home, with proper nights and plenty of traffic. Well, I had time to figure out a solution.

It began to rain. The fog thickened. I wrapped myself up and slept for an hour.

37

It had all become absurdly easy. Mooching around in the north-west corner of the Barents Sea, more than a month out from Whitehills, with a couple of thousand miles in our wake, there was little work to do, little to worry about and, apart from the occasional shooting pain in my feet, little discomfort. The smaller details of each day were different, of course, but the general pattern was the same: sleep, eat, navigate, raise sail, take in sail, adjust the self-steering gear, write up the ship's log and my personal log, sit in the hatchway and observe what little could be seen of the world. It was all very subdued and civilised. If the wind did not blow, I was happy to lie becalmed with the sail bundle lashed tightly to the boom gallows. Should it blow up hard I was content to reduce sail and forereach gently along under a single panel or less. Neither extreme posed any particular threat or concern, as long as I ensured that we always had a suitable offing from any hazard. My ease and relaxation were founded on two principles: firstly not being overly concerned about speed; secondly not being overly concerned about the fine detail of my route. The need always to be getting on, thereby forcing the pace beyond what is optimum for boat and crew, creates stress and tiredness; a rigidly fixed itinerary can soon become a kind of tyranny, especially for the engineless sailor. To be ever pliant in the matter of where one goes, and the speed at which one goes there, brings one more into harmony with the natural forces one is harnessing. Voyaging becomes a gentle waltz rather than a head-on battle.

As I lay there and thought about the voyage so far, it seemed to me that it had given and withheld in about equal measure. I had managed to achieve the general shape and the principal objectives. This was never a given, and so I was grateful for that. I had been frustrated, though, in some of the finer detail: a headwind had forced us away from the north coast of Svalbard; Franz Josef Land had remained invisible; Cape Fligely had turned out to be a risk too far. The balance was fair, though, and I had no complaints.

There was a third element too that contributed to the general absence of any stress or anxiety – my total confidence in *Mingming II*. She was as close as I could reasonably expect get to my ideal ship: compact, strong, totally watertight, easy and safe to manage. She was, in a word, supremely *reassuring*. As I have argued many times, the great advantage of a modestly sized boat is that there is never any threat of the forces exerted on or by her becoming too large to control. There was nothing in the rig that could not be handled by means of a simple block and tackle; everything was on a scale that matched my own limited strength and stature. The equation of increased size with increased reassurance is one which I have never found convincing. The bigger the boat, the more diminutive and potentially helpless the crew; the greater the possibility of being physically overwhelmed should something break or misfunction. For a lowly single-hander, *Mingming II* seemed to me to be the ideal compromise: long enough on the waterline and well-enough canvassed to maintain an adequate pace; roomy enough to provide more than enough basic comfort and stowage space; compact enough to retain a good strength-for-weight ratio, high rigidity and supremely easy manageability. And with no reliance on any form of sophisticated technology (apart from the single electrical circuit to power my navigation lights – the one thing which had failed on the voyage so far, a fact whose irony was not lost on me), I was always relaxed in the matter of potential problems. Given the excess of so-called redundant strength in the hull and rig, I knew that any major failure was unlikely, but I was also confident that given the simplicity of the structure, I would be able to fix anything that did go wrong.

One area in which I had compromised a reluctance to embrace technologies that were beyond my power to control or fix was that of navigation. During this voyage in particular I had become more dependent than I would have liked on my hand-held GPS for position-fixing. This weighed on me somewhat, almost to the point of feeling slightly guilty every time I switched the damned thing on, which except in tight coastal situations was no more than once every twenty-four hours. It was a reliance which I disliked intensely, but one which was largely foisted on me by this voyage's relentless asolarity (a word which I coined in the middle of the Barents Sea, meaning 'absence of sun', but which has yet to make its appearance in the Oxford English Dictionary). My sextant had, for most of the voyage, lain unused in its box, simply because the sun, moon, stars and anything remotely heaven-bound had remained almost permanently invisible. It was impossible in those conditions to navigate celestially in any meaningful way. This is not to say that had my GPS, and its spare, failed, or had the satellite system been switched off or disabled in some way, I would have been in some kind of navigational crisis. Far from it. Using the time-honoured skills of dead reckoning, allied with all the other 'bare-foot' rules of thumb, I could have kept us moving safely until such time as the sun reappeared. I would not necessarily, however, have sailed the same route. For example, I would probably have chosen the tack that took us south into the clear waters of the Barents Sea rather than the one which brought us west and in close to the islands of Kong Karls Land. There was more than enough ocean at my disposal to have coped without GPS. I could therefore justify my use of it by describing it as a reliance by choice rather than by necessity. It simply allowed me to cut things more finely and approach coastlines that I otherwise would have kept even more clear of. This was a weak excuse, I knew, that perhaps masked a certain level of laziness.

One result of this insistent asolarity (a word whose usage has now already doubled since its first appearance in the English language) was an even greater respect, on my part, for the whalers and sealers who had worked these waters for centuries with only the most rudimentary navigational equipment. In summers as overcast and fog-laden as the one I was experiencing, it was a mystery to me how they coped. Of course very often they didn't; the rates of ship loss and human mortality were high.

This was another reminder of the softness of the modern age. The Royal Navy no longer sends fourteen-year-olds through the pack-ice in command of open boats. We may not necessarily lament this, seeing it, through the contemporary prism, as a form of child labour. On the other hand, it produced officers who by the age of twenty had a wealth of genuinely tough and worldly experience, a comprehensive knowledge of their trade, and no illusions about the knife-edge of survival atop whose sweetly-honed and indiscriminate blade we journey through our short span.

38

The north-eastern limit of the Edgeøya ice cliffs is defined by a right-angled shoulder, Cape Melchers. To its south, the ice cliffs stretch for thirty miles or so; to its west and north, the ice cliffs carry on for just a few miles before metamorphosing into the usual rocky talus which curves round to the north-north west, creating a large, shallow, but potentially dangerous bay. In 2014 we had touched lightly on the south-east corner of this bay, but now, with the winds from the east, it was not a place I cared to revisit. Nor did I have any appetite for coming in too close to the ice cliffs south of Cape Melchers. In 2014 there had been a procession of floes, created by ice falling off the cliffs, making its way north close in to the coast. With an onshore wind and a high prevalence of fog I had no intention of making a close acquaintance with that procession.

By five in the morning of Saturday the fourth of August, our thirty-fourth day at sea, we were about eleven miles to the north-east of Cape Melchers. There was of course no sign of the Cape, or of the ice-back of Edgeøya, in the persistent mist. With the wind backing a little, I hardened up to head due south, parallel with the frozen Edgeøya coastline. There was still considerable doubt in my mind as to whether we would be able to pass to windward of the group of small islands now about ten miles slightly west of south of us – the Ryke Yseøyane, or Ryke Yse Islands, named for the Dutch whaler who discovered them in the mid-seventeenth century. In 2014 we had passed well to the inside of them; they had been no more than low dark smudges on the eastern horizon. Now they lay more or less on our track, depending on whether the wind decided to back or veer, and how well we could keep up to it. If possible I preferred to pass to windward, as I did not want to bear off and reduce our offing from the main coast for no good reason. The rule of thumb is always to steal a bit to windward if possible.

The wind backed a little more and by mid-morning there they were, fine on the starboard bow: three or four long slabs of low-lying rock, perhaps no more than seventy or eighty feet high; black, bare, supremely desolate. With the wind holding and what seemed to be a south-going current helping us along, we skirted down their eastern side just a mile or two off. Here was rock eroded and weathered almost back into the sea, planed and smoothed to utter featurelessness. The only interruption to the unblemished contour lines of both of the bigger islands were, on each of them, a small rectangular obtrusion that almost anywhere else would have been taken for some kind of building. That seemed so unlikely that I assumed that they were just chance rock formations. I recalled the church I had seen sitting on a headland on the west coast of Jan Mayen, a church which was so convincing that I could almost hear the plainsong drifting over the water from it, until the light and our position changed, transforming the illusion to its more mundane reality.

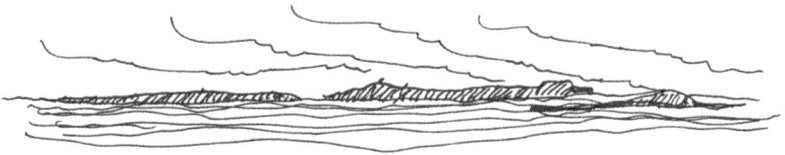

The Ryke Yseøyane from East c. 2 miles

The wind backed a little further and so I eased the mainsheet a little to keep us heading due south towards the island of Hopen. As the evening advanced I began to notice some subtle changes. For the first time in several weeks there was a hint of real night descending. We were still to the north of 77°North, and so still more than six hundred and fifty miles inside the Arctic Circle, but our twenty-four hour daylight, the great joy of the High Arctic in summer, was already under threat. Offsetting this was a sudden surge in warmth. The temperature aboard *Mingming II* is determined as much by that of the sea as that of the air, and there was no question that we were now moving into warmer water. My hands and feet were still painful, but the sharpness of the pangs was slowly easing. What was left was a kind of permanent low-grade pins and needles mixed with occasional numbness. It would be weeks before it cleared completely.

Other things were unchanged. Rain alternated with thick fog. Rain combined with thick fog. The horizon was as forlorn as ever. Somewhere beyond it the Infernal Fug Factory was still hard at work belching out an endless stream of murk, a trillion cubic metres an hour, on and on, day after day, week after week, relentlessly suffocating the world in a pall of impenetrable grey. Looking skywards I saw nothing but a reflection of a silver-grey sea. We were pinned between moist pewter air and a wet pewter ocean. All was wetness and greyness, an oppressive tunnel from which there was no escape and, it seemed, never would be.

I had little optimism that we would see much of Hopen. The wind had backed to the north-east and strengthened, and so we were racing firmly along under two panels, the wind now on the port quarter. By five the next morning we were little more than eight miles to the north-west of the northern end of the island. I kept a good watch, not just for the land close by, but for walruses: it was hereabouts that we had encountered a small herd four years previously, much to my surprise. There was little logic in supposing that they might still be hanging around, on the lookout for passing yachts, but I clung on to the notion all the same, conscious that this might well be my last chance to see them, ever.

I wondered about this strange and now almost universal impulsion to see things. There was no question that having seen, for example, the Seven Islands, I somehow felt a little more complete; some need had been satisfied.

Watching out for walruses, I considered the fact that in all my time in the Arctic, I had never seen a polar bear. This was of course a function of the way I navigate, given that polar bears frequent ice and land, both of which I try to keep clear of. *Do you see polar bears?* is almost invariably the first question I am asked in relation to my Arctic voyages. It would be nice to be able to reply: *Oh, of course! All the time! They often try and climb aboard the boat. I once fended one off with the steering oar!* That would make me a real Arctic hand. I can always sense a slight disappointment when I reply: *No. Never.* Seeing things somehow enhances personal worth and credibility.

I thought about other things I had never seen. Bow-head whales. Belugas. Narwhals. Franz Josef Land. Ivory Gulls. Eskimos. My Arctic checklist was still woefully incomplete. This did not bother me in the least. I had long since learned to treasure the gifts which had been granted rather than to yearn for those which had not. I was no better or worse a man for not having seen a polar bear or a narwhal. Besides, the Arctic had taught me more than I could ever have anticipated: acceptance, equanimity and the raw beauty of ineluctable transience.

39

Just before six in the morning the north cape of Hopen, Hope Island, no more than a hazy dark shadow topped with low cloud, insinuated itself into the murk on our port bow. Its visibility was not constant in the swirling cloud and mist; occasionally it faded almost out of view; occasionally a patch of clearer air allowed it depth and solidity. We were just a few miles off, but after a while the island disappeared entirely once again.

North Cape of Hopen under Cloud from West c.7miles

We ran south-south-east, parallel with the long slug of high rock that comprises the island. Tired after a night without much sleep, and cold from a protracted stay at the hatchway,

I relaxed my self-discipline, polishing off a substantial piece of fruit and nut chocolate and washing it down with a mug of hot bouillon. So close to land, sleep was of course inadmissible, and so I once more took up my vigil at the hatch.

It was the English whaler, walrus hunter, explorer and general ruffian Thomas Marmaduke of Hull who had named the island, after his former ship the *Hopewell.* He had sailed extensively around this area in the early seventeenth century and is said to have had designs on finding a north-east passage.

Hopen, it would seem, is the Brünnich's guillemot capital of the world, the place where any self-respecting guillemot that wants to make its way on the world just has to be. Great squadrons of the birds whirred past in a breathless stream. Each bird carried a small fish or sand eel in its bill, racing home to feed baby Giles or little Gillian, driven on by the mindless genetic imperative. More than any other seabird I know, it is the Brünnich's guillemot that invites constant anthropomorphic metaphor. Maybe it is something about the clean-cut nature of its dinner-suited plumage allied with the purposefulness of its flight. The flocks of birds zipping by put me in mind of conventions of bankers, advertising executives, lobbyists, accountants, political aspirants, hedge fund managers, motivational speakers, insurance brokers, property salesmen, corporate lawyers, football pundits, barristers, money men and mobsters. I could almost smell the after-shave. Here were the captains of great guillemot industries going about the most important of business with an unflinching zeal. There was something quasi-comical in their earnestness and unquestioning self-importance, just as there is something quasi-comical in the earnestness and unquestioning self-importance of their human counterparts. The convergences were too obvious to overlook.

Hopen appeared again. From time to time I could make out the low points on the island that divide its ridge into a series of separate coffins, or sausages, or railway carriages; six high plateaus linked by shallow declivities. It was odd to know that I was close to human life once more: there is a manned radio station on the east side of the island. It did not occur to me to try to call it up on my hand-held VHF radio. I was happy to pass by incognito.

An Iceland gull, perhaps the most poised and elegant of the larger gulls, attached itself to us for a while and escorted us down the coastline. Its procedure was to land fifty yards or so in front of us, slightly to the side of our trajectory, watch us pass, and wait until we were a few hundred yards ahead before taking off and repeating the sequence. About the same size as a herring gull, but pure white except for its light-grey upper wing feathers, more slender-winged and graceful, it flew with an unhurried, almost languid, ease. Once settled on the water it maintained a perfect pose, its shapely neck held aloft at all times, as if aware of the beauty of its form. The bird exuded supreme calmness and self-containment; its presence was somehow restful. After an hour or so it grew tired of the game, or found other distractions, and left us to sail on alone.

By midday the south cape of Hopen, Kapp Thor, little more than an abrupt dark smudge, lay square on our port beam. Four years earlier ice floes had been grounded in the shallow water to its west; now there was nothing. I wondered how the island's extensive polar bear population was faring in these changing conditions. So many life forms are being whittled away, inexorably. It is noble to want to save them, but is it misconceived to attempt to hold back the juggernaut of change and causality? Death and renewal is the law of nature. Species come and go. The endgame will play itself out regardless.

The wind fell away and for a while we rolled uncomfortably with the sail slatting in its usual noisy way. I suspected this was what I call the headland effect, as Kapp Thor was now almost to windward. Capes and high cliffs play havoc with the wind, creating holes and squalls. Sure enough, within half an hour the breeze, now in the east-north-east, had resumed its normal steadiness. We pulled away from the island, bound now for the eastern side of Bear Island, a hundred and fifty miles to our south-east. Clear of the land, I could think once more about sleep. I stretched out below and slept, for two hours, the light but reviving sleep of the lone sailor.

40

Since rounding the top of the Seven Islands we had amassed a catalogue of close encounters with the islands of Franz Josef Land and eastern Svalbard, working our dogged way along and around, down and about, but had seen little more than a distant whaleback of ice and the occasional shoulder of rock. It had been a kind of Blind Man's Buff, with just enough touching to confirm that the terrestrial world had not deserted us completely. We were now nearing the end of this blinkered tour of these remote islands. Ahead, across the shallow waters of the Spitsbergen Banks, lay the final landmark before we departed definitively to the south and home.

In 2014 we had angled out to the south-west and Jan Mayen, avoiding Bear Island completely; this time Bear Island lay so close to our ideal track as to be almost unavoidable. I aimed to pass down its eastern side, as this would bring us past the South Cape, the ideal point for taking our departure, without any deviation from our course.

When I woke from my sleep, Hopen's Kapp Thor had long since fallen away into the mist. It was now the time to increase my vigilance; the last time I had crossed the Spitsbergen banks I had seen a fishing boat or two at work.

At ten thirty that evening we crossed 76°North. As is my habit I awarded myself a Fox's Glacier Mint to celebrate the achievement. Perhaps just as significantly, our longitude from the Greenwich meridian had already halved since we had turned back at 46°East. I had never developed the custom of rewarding myself on the basis of longitude, in retrospect something of an oversight; at a sweet per degree I could already have consumed a whole packet and felt quite virtuous about it too.

The Spitsbergen Banks brought no relief from the overcast. The night darkened. It rained again. The wind eased and we rolled noisily. Our flock of escorting fulmars increased in number, perhaps associating us, in their dim brains, with a bountiful fishing boat. The wind backed towards the north and eased even more. I switched to the other downwind tack to give us more westing. The wind carried on backing, right round to the north-west and, as usually happens when it reaches that vigorous quadrant, blew up more strongly. I reduced the sail to just two panels and we sped across the Banks, homeward bound with a bone in our teeth. We were into our thirty-sixth day at sea. A Pomarine skua flew past, followed by a long-tailed skua and two little auks.

Just after midnight I went to the hatch to readjust the self-steering gear. Making my usual scan of the horizon I picked up a faint white triangle to the north-west. A sail! I retrieved the binoculars from their hook beside the companionway and studied the apparition as best I could in the heaving sea. The yacht was hull down, heading northwards on an almost reciprocal course to our own. Judging by the size of the sail it was a big craft, maybe an expedition yacht of some sort.

It was unlikely that even the sharpest-eyed watchkeeper on board would have seen us down on their leeward horizon. We would be hull down too, and with just two panels of the grey sail set low down, were probably showing nothing but the top half of a grey-painted municipal lamp post, shorn of its light fitting and heading slowly south-west. Our opposite courses were taking us quickly away from each other, so I did not bother assembling the hand-held VHF to see if I could make contact with them. Their position indicated that having left Bear Island they were bound for the eastern side of Spitsbergen, rather than taking the usual route up the west coast. Maybe they were heading for Franz Josef Land. Well, I hoped they would have better visibility than had been our lot.

If the crew of the yacht were optimistic about their likely weather, it was not, at that moment, without good reason: looking to the north I could see, for what seemed like the first time in weeks, a wide expanse of blue sky. The northbound yacht might possibly be sailing into the limpid and sun-drenched conditions we had been denied. Seeing that crystal-clear air astern I could easily have surrendered to a regretful indulgence of the 'if only' and 'what if' kind. I refused the temptation, not wishing to surrender my tranquillity to something as capricious as meteorological change. I could do nothing about the weather, but everything about how I reacted to it.

The cloud overhead started to break up a little, allowing short bursts of proper sunshine. The cabin warmed a little. I hoped that the sunshine might give a boost to the recalcitrant battery. Sizable flocks of kittiwakes streamed past high above us, they too heading landwards. We crossed 75°North and I unwrapped another mint.

The visibility was the best it had a been for a while but I refused to trust it. At four-thirty in the afternoon the upper slopes of Bear Island's highest mountains, the Miseryfellet, loomed up fine on the starboard bow. Well, there it was once again, Bear Island, in all probability the last land we would see until Shetland or possibly even the Moray coastline. Four long-tailed skuas made their way to windward in quick succession, and as I studied the distant expanse of rock ahead I realised, without the least surprise, that a blanket of haze was starting to wrap itself around the island. By ten in the evening we ourselves were once more into fog. Bear Island had, of course, disappeared.

41

The crew, that unspeakable rabble, had settled into a kind of semi-comatose resignation. The voyage was progressing with such order and uneventfulness that there was little for them to do, and so they mouldered away, each one wrapped in his own morbid preoccupation.

The Ship's Doctor *and* Dentist for example, having rightly decided that the amputation of a troublesome toe was a little beyond his skill level, and having further discovered that there was little in the way of pills or potions to prescribe for what were, in any case, no more than trivial ailments, had retired to his narrow berth, where he dreamed of pulling off great and unlikely medical triumphs. What these were, he had no idea, but he could already see his portrait, subtly lit and showing his best profile, on the cover of the *Lancet*. Maybe, just maybe, a knighthood might be coming his way, or perhaps a keynote speech at the British Medical Association conference. He mulled long and hard over the title of his address. *Cold Comfort: Advances in Arctic Pathologies* sounded pretty good, although he still had to figure out what those advances were, and perhaps needed to check exactly what the word 'pathologies' meant. Maybe he could adopt a more personal and upbeat tone: *North Pole Doctor: How I Kept the Crew Alive!* That had a certain ring to it, and should ensure a good attendance, although he was slightly troubled by the fact that the crew seemed to have kept themselves alive without too much professional help.

The Ship's Collector of Rain, dismayed that so far he had not once been required to apply his considerable (in his estimation) skills, plotted the legal evisceration of his hated skipper. He had been shipped aboard under false pretences and he was going to make the bastard pay. He lay in his dark corner and dredged up from the depths of his memory everything he knew about the law of employment, the law of contract, the law of defamation, the law of libel, in short the law of anything and everything he could think of, preparing his case with a clinical and gleeful precision. He wanted his skipper up before the court, sued silly for everything under the sun; exposed, humiliated and ruined. He smiled to himself as he imagined the scene: the Old Bailey, of course; the packed Press Gallery; the public benches filled to capacity; the shaking skipper, handcuffed, head hung, standing mournfully in the dock, cut down to size at last, reduced to a pitiful nonentity, a bag of abject misery; and the moment of triumph: the Judge's gavel descending with a resounding thud as the word echoed around the land: *Guilty!*

That snivelling wretch of a Cabin Boy, who by now had grown too old, too hormone-charged for that time-honoured calling, was no less mutinous than the rest of them. Pimply and love-sick, he passed the hours in lascivious fantasising. If I had any sympathy for any of the misfits and failures that comprised the crew, it was for him. The poor lad really wasn't cut out for ascetism, self-denial or Stoic indifference. He knew achingly well what he wanted to do, and who he wanted to do it with. Being cooped up with a load of taciturn and embittered old geezers, while knowing that at that very moment the object of his desire might be succumbing to the bestial charms of some shelf-stacker from Tesco, was, for him, as good a Dantean hell as it was possible to construct.

That left the latest addition to the sad complement – the Ship's Distributor of Nuts. At least he had something constructive to do twice a day, but despite his regular occupation, he excelled at introducing the greatest joylessness into what could, in other hands, have been the occasion for levity, even conviviality. The generally held opinion was that he was a merciless sod with a heart of stone. Not one extra sunflower seed, not one shrivelled currant, let alone anything as monumental as a whole almond or a plump and sticky date, ever escaped his fingers unintentionally. He was insensible to any sort of appeal, as ironbound as a Navy Bosun doling out the daily tot. *That's your ration, sunshine. Take it or leave it.* Those long and agile fingers of his, whose hygiene seemed to deteriorate as each day passed, and which invariably promised so much more than they delivered, had become an object of fascinated hatred amongst the crew. There was no question that the man took a sadistic pleasure in plunging his hand deep into the trail mix, filling his wide palm to overflowing, thereby raising expectations and bringing on a sudden rush of salivation in the mouths of his hungry onlookers, before depositing the final miserable pittance onto the waiting plate. The trouble was, the man's lack of compassion had a solid rationale. He knew better than any of us that if anything went wrong, protracting our time at sea, his current niggardliness might end up being a lifesaver. This gave him a moral superiority that made him even more unbearable.

As skipper of this disparate collection of sociopaths my

work was cut out to maintain some kind of constructive harmony. I didn't bother with the usual props of man management: bonding sessions, five-a-side football, building bridges across fast-flowing streams, community singing, that kind of thing, preferring to leave each man brooding but undisturbed in his shady lair, where he could do the least damage to himself and to everyone else on board.

42

By midnight, well-wrapped in the usual murk, we were running down the east side of Bear Island, about twelve miles off. In the final analysis, it made no difference whether I managed to get a look at the island itself or not, but despite the trail of unseen land astern and my growing unconcern at the level of bounty we were or were not accorded, something still kept me at the hatch, peering westwards into the gloom.

At about three in the morning my perseverance was rewarded. A patch of thick cloud lifted a little, revealing a dark stain of grainy talus. The wind had backed into the west and with the help of a healthy south-going current we were now racing along, eating up the miles that would take us clear of the island and out into the Norwegian Sea once more. It was not long before I could make out the southern extremity, South Cape, with its unmistakable needle of rock just a little way offshore. The green slopes which top the cape, and which had entranced me on my first visit here four years previously, were drowned in the low cloud. The mist was forever swirling around, bringing the land in and out of view. Overhead the cloud was thinning a little, but around the island itself it remained resolutely thick. Another Iceland gull adopted us for a short while. Astern, for the first time on the voyage, one of the massive cigar-shaped clouds which stretch from horizon to horizon, which seem only to appear in the Arctic, and which I had dubbed *Hindenburgus arcticus,* formed itself within just a few minutes. A moment or two later it was gone, having melted back into the featureless stratum of vapour from which it had materialised.

As we came level with the South Cape, I hardened up a little to bring us closer to the wind and onto our direct track for Whitehills, some thirteen hundred miles away. With the land still there, I was not yet ready to indulge the surge of expectation that always accompanies the moment of departure on a long passage. Even though we had been at sea for well over a month, I knew I would still feel a renewed sense of liberation once we pulled away definitively, and quite possibly for the last time, from Bear Island. It was not just Bear Island that we were leaving, but Svalbard itself. Thinking back over the voyage so far, I realised that had we passed to the east, rather than the west, of Hopen, we would now have circumnavigated the entire Svalbard group, every single rock and island. This had never occurred to me as an objective when planning the voyage, no doubt because of the wealth of unknowns and uncertainties that clouded our potential route. I wondered whether, had I been aware of what was at stake, I would have altered course slightly to encompass Hopen. Well, I will never know the answer to that question. The thought of having sailed around the entire group may well have brought on a rush of pleasure. On the other hand, I was acutely aware that in the larger scheme of things it would have been a trivial accomplishment, adding precisely nothing to the sum of anything, barring my own petty self-satisfaction.

Last View of Bjørnøya from SSE c.10 miles

By nine in the morning the South Cape of Bear Island was starting to fade into the ever-evolving fog. An occasional dark patch showed through before it was gone forever. As we pulled away from the land I realised that Olga, usually so strident whenever we were close to Bear Island, had remained silent. No telephone calls. No messages in bottles. Nothing. Had she given up on me? Had she been rescued and carried off by someone else? Had she made the ultimate sacrifice for nature, and allowed herself to be eaten by a polar bear? I would never know, but I felt a certain sadness, whatever her fate. Despite her persistence and her misconceptions, for I never was a *good-breeding Englishman and banking at Coutts*, I had grown fond of her from the very moment when I had almost read the message she had so courageously sent to me, secreted inside that dark green bottle floating across the Norwegian Sea. With her long blonde hair, blue eyes and endearing tantrums, she had become a permanent presence aboard. Even now I can still hear her voice carrying across the waves: *Englishman, you come rescue me! Right now!*

43

Under four panels, with a steady breeze out of the west, we began the final phase of the voyage. By noon our total distance run, on the basis of our straight-line noon-to-noon positions, was two thousand, three hundred and fifty-four nautical miles. In reality was had probably covered well over two and a half thousand miles so far. Over two thirds of the voyage was complete. Despite that, and despite the fact that we had a long stretch of open and empty ocean ahead of us, devoid of hazards, I was not complacent. Far from it. I knew that the last leg would be long and hard. We would soon be moving away from the benign weather of the Arctic summer and back into the muscular band dominated by the Jetstream. The likelihood was that low-pressure systems would pile in, one after the other, in a relentless onslaught. The fact that it was still only August was unlikely to provide any relief; severe and unstable weather, with a predominance of south-westerly wind, was still a distinct possibility. We would be heading straight into the North Atlantic Current as well.

The weather did not take long to assert itself. By late that evening we were down to just one panel of the sail. Rain squalls lashed us from time to time. Hungry after a night and day of disruptions, I cooked my dinner an hour earlier than usual and slept for a while.

By morning the wind had veered to the north-west and eased considerably. For the first time in weeks I was able to dispense with the heavy fleece top layer I had been wearing. Gloves, too, were no longer necessary. I kept my moonboots on, though; it was not yet the time to revert to the woollen knitted slippers I usually wear at sea.

Throughout the day the wind fell away and the air grew more balmy. In the smoothing sea I applied myself to various housekeeping tasks: checking over torches and batteries in anticipation of the proper nights to come; transferring food stowed away under the cockpit well into the immediately accessible forward containers. I started examining the wiring of the solar control panel to see if there was some way of circumventing the so-called 'load disconnect', the part of the apparatus that automatically disables the battery if it thinks the voltage is too low. During the occasional spell of sunshine the green light had come on again, only to revert to red as soon as the conditions had darkened. I knew that the battery was healthy, just not quite healthy enough to satisfy the high standards of whoever had designed the control panel. It was frustrating to know that there was enough charge there to power my navigation lights, but that the use of that charge was being denied because of the design of the system. Looking at all the connections I concluded that it would be possible to re-connect the solar panel directly to the battery, thereby excluding the automatic cut-out. I decided to see how the battery fared as we went south. If it did not recharge adequately to satisfy the control panel, I now had a way of solving the dilemma.

It was rare for me to have to confront this kind of technical problem. In the main I could sail on, day after day, without the least worry about anything going wrong. I could therefore give myself up to the pure experience, the movement through time and space, the feel and sounds of a simple structure harnessing the unseen energy of the wind. I could live right in the primitive moment, enjoying the raw aliveness without an overlay of sapping calculation. The great gift of simplicity and robustness was freedom from the least anxiety. To sail thus, carefree and light of mind, brought the act closer to something that might be called transcendence. That is a grand word, for sure, which ought not be used lightly or loosely. What I mean is that weeks of constant motion, of effortless and relaxed propulsion, can bewitch and liberate the psyche, allowing it to float free. One can be brought to another place, another person. To have to think too much about things like wires and electrical circuits can quickly destroy the poetry of the journey. The whole point of the design of *Mingming II* was to use careful forethought in order to be able, once at sea, to exclude concern for the merely technical; to overcome it, relegate it, suppress it, and so leave the spirit free. It took me a while, therefore, and a conscious effort of will, to bring myself down to the point where I could examine the wretched solar control panel and work out what I needed to do to override its intractable system. I really did not want to be bothered with that sort of nonsense, fiddling about with screw drivers and connections, trying to sustain the viability of a dimly understood circuitry. It had to be done, though, however much it rankled; I needed working lights for the final stages of the voyage.

The wind slowly faded and by nine-thirty that evening we were once more becalmed. For the first time since Kvitöya, now four hundred and fifty miles astern, I dropped and lashed the sail. It was a fitful night. Sometimes I slept. Once or twice I managed to coax a little forward motion from an uncertain zephyr from the east-north-east. I enjoyed the lightness and freedom of movement that came with wearing fewer clothes. It was warm enough now for me to be able to leave the after hatch open. We were still above 72°North, and therefore nearly four hundred miles within the Arctic Circle, but such are the effects of acclimatization; for the moment the air felt soft and spring-like.

Our noon position put us less than a thousand miles from Whitehills. Just after lunch I made a symbolic change of wardrobe, taking off my moonboots and reverting to slippers. This simple act sealed the fact that we were now out of the High Arctic. A faint breeze came up once more, and as the afternoon progressed, so too did we, haltingly, with the occasional gybe in the light and shifting air from astern. I knelt in the after hatch, enjoying the new-found warmth, and watched the world receding slowly astern. From time to time milky sunshine pierced the cloud. Had I been a cat I might well have purred with the pleasure of the moment.

44

It was the ancient Greeks who first identified, named and delved deep into the concept they called *hubris*. It came to form a central element of their Tragedies. The man who committed *hubris*, believing himself, by virtue of excessive pride and self-confidence, to be the equal of, or even better than, the Gods, thus paved the way for his own inescapable downfall, his *nemesis*.

The lone sailor flirts constantly with this duality, though he or she may not know or recognise it. The ocean is not man's natural element; to spend so much time upon it, alone and unaided, flies somewhat in the face of Nature. The very fact of being there might suggest reckless self-confidence; a disdain for the Gods and the order they have set upon the world. The solo sailor had better watch out! This constant and shameless provocation of the Deities will sooner or later lead to some form of retribution. The Gods have ways of dealing with those who get above themselves.

For the whole of the afternoon I knelt comfortably in the after hatch, my knees cushioned on the broad main step, my mind relaxed and unfocused, idly enjoying the satisfactions of a voyage which so far had been as well-made as I could have hoped for. Patches of open sky here and there turned the sea to a deep blue; the breeze was gentle; the faint swell and the easy roll of the boat lulled me to a kind of waking reverie.

After some hours in this benign state it occurred to me that I really ought to check the horizon ahead. It was all very well to while away the time watching our wake, but it hardly constituted good watchkeeping. I left my position in the after hatch and went below to have a look through the forward windows of the observation pod. Not far ahead, on our starboard bow, a dark blue Iberian-style fishing boat was trawling eastwards, towards our track. Having only seen a single yacht hull-down during the course of several weeks of sailing, it gave me something of a jolt to be so close to another vessel again.

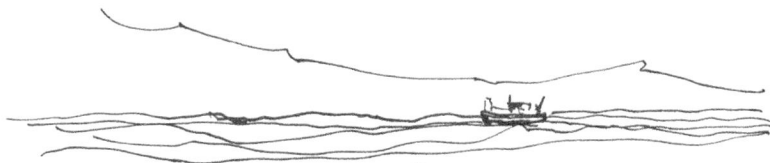

Dark Blue Fishing Boat

Nonetheless I felt pretty pleased with myself. Although I could have dreamed on for another hour or two, my natural seamanship had taken over, interrupting my trance and forcing me to check all round. I had re-asserted one of the basic principles of navigation: *always look where you are going.* I wondered whether the time had come for me to write a book on the subject, a kind of definitive guide for navigators, incorporating this kind of basic knowledge which I had acquired over the years. I put that thought aside for the moment, as I had the fishing boat to attend to.

I unhooked the self-steering chain from the tiller and took over control of the boat, bearing away to pass well astern of the trawler. At that point the fishing boat, about half a mile ahead of us, turned through a hundred and eighty degrees and steamed off west. I hardened up again, back to our original course. I kept on hand-steering, keeping my eye firmly on the fishing boat. It was clearly working some sort of pattern and might well come back towards us again. In the light and fickle wind we would be unable to take rapid avoiding action, so I needed to track its movements constantly, the better to make early decisions for avoidance.

And so I watched it, relentlessly, peering to starboard round the back of the sprayhood, congratulating myself on my alertness and on my understanding of the way fishing boats worked their grids. My concentration on the trawler never wavered, even as it moved further away to the west. I did not trust it and would not let it out of my sight until we were well past it. I wondered about assembling my hand-held VHF radio, in case I needed to call it up, but decided not to relinquish the tiller for even a moment. A good seaman does not waste time in idle chat; he attends to the business of the sea. The trawler turned south, parallel with our course. I suspected that it might continue its turn and come back our way but instead it seemed to stop. It was now pretty much square on our starboard beam, a good distance away. With luck we might now be out of danger.

I congratulated myself on a job well done; we would soon be able to settle back to our previous course. Before long I would be able to hook up the self-steering again and think at more length about all the advice I could give to less experienced and less competent navigators. It seemed that the least I could do was share my knowledge and expertise with those in need of it.

At that moment we lurched to a sudden halt. It was an uncanny sensation, in the middle of an empty ocean, to feel the boat suddenly held back, as if a giant hand had grabbed hold of the central keel and stopped us in our tracks. The mainsail was drawing nicely but we were going nowhere. I dragged my eyes away from the fishing boat I had been following for so long and peered forward around the side of the sprayhood. Hard against our starboard side was a huge bright red buoy. Another big red buoy was straining against our port bow. Further to port was a danbuoy with a tattered flag, followed by a line of five small white buoys and, at the east end of this motley parade, another large red buoy. Bloody hell! We had sailed straight into a collection of closely spaced buoys and their interconnecting ropes. There were nine buoys in all, an exemplary and highly visible array. In the wide expanse of the Norwegian Sea, I had nailed them perfectly.

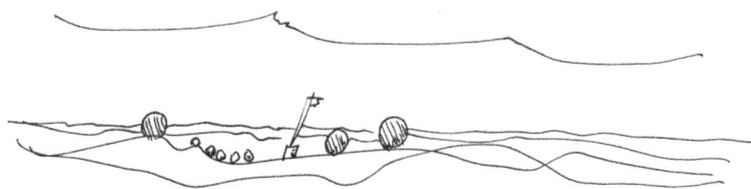

An Exemplary Array of Buoys

Not bothering with my rule of always wearing an attached harness on deck, I scrambled out of the hatch and went partly forward, peering over the side to see what was going on under the surface. A baroque cat's cradle of highly tensioned green polypropylene ropes led from the buoys down into the depths. One of these lines was hard against the forward end of the keel. I had sailed right into the end of the fishing boat's net.

As if to prove the maxim that one human error almost invariably leads to another, I then made a very bad and ill-considered decision. I figured that if I could push the line down below the keel, we would thus be released and sail on unimpeded. I dived below for the boathook, came back on deck and tried to force the line down under the bottom of the keel. Fortunately, I could not do it. The end of the boathook could not grip the line adequately and there was just too much tension on the rope anyway. For a moment or two I was flummoxed. I wondered whether the trawler had seen me sail onto its buoys. Might I have to ask for help to get me off? Jesus, what a mess!

We were still straining against the line, and I finally did what I ought to have done straight away. I dropped the sail. The north-going current eased us back off the array and into clear water. Within a few seconds we were free. I let us drift back until we were well away from the buoys before raising the sail and resuming our course.

Yes indeed, *hubris* had brought me to *nemesis*. In my confidence I had neglected the cardinal rule: I had not been looking where we were going. The possibility of another hazard besides the fishing boat had not crossed my mind. It was so basic that I felt thoroughly ashamed of myself. Moreover, by not thinking carefully before reacting, I could have made things much worse. It is obvious what would have happened had I managed to push the rope which was holding us far enough down to pass under the keel. With the tension that was on it, it would immediately have popped up again between the aft end of the keel and the rudder skeg. We then would have been absolutely and inextricably caught. We would have been unable to go forward or back, and the integrity of the skeg and the rudder would have been under serious threat. The possible outcome did not bear too much thinking about.

I sailed on, annoyed with myself, chastened, embarrassed, but also mightily relieved that it had not turned out worse.

Perhaps it was not quite yet the time to write the definitive treatise on advanced seamanship.

I pondered on the probabilities of sailing into a hazard perhaps six yards wide in that empty ocean. Had I been trying to keep to an accurate course, sailing down a trajectory just one nautical mile wide, the chances of hitting the buoys would have been three hundred and thirty-three to one. Those odds were low enough, but I was in fact sailing much more loosely. I was meandering down a broad swathe of ocean with an east-west tolerance of at least twenty nautical miles. In that case the odds of hitting the buoys rose to almost seven thousand to one. I had scored a commendable bull's eye.

I remembered that at one point I had considered calling up the fishing boat. Now I imagined how the conversation might have gone:

Good afternoon, sir, and if I may say so, a jolly fine afternoon it is too.

Hey you! Crazy guy in stupid sailboat! You keep out my way, man! I fishing! Don't want no stupid sailboat messing up my fish!

No problem, sir. I have had you in sight for a long while now. I am taking all the necessary evasive actions and keeping a very, very good watch.

OK, but you stupid sailboat guys always doing stupid things!

Sir, you can trust me implicitly. I am a thoroughly experienced seaman and once even had a short article published in Yachting Monthly. My word is my bond, sir. I promise I will in no way interfere with your exemplary fishing operation.

It would have been about then that I ran into his exemplary array of buoys.

45

We carried on south, but now the wind was dropping away. At nine in the evening I lowered and lashed the sail. The fishing boat had fallen below the northern horizon but I could still hear the low hum of its engines. That faint undertone kept me on edge: the current was carrying back northwards, back towards danger. Well, there was nothing I could do about it.

It began to rain, gently at first, then harder. We heaved imperceptibly to the faintest of swells. I slept in short bursts, my mind still focussed on the trawler working back and forth just a few miles to our north.

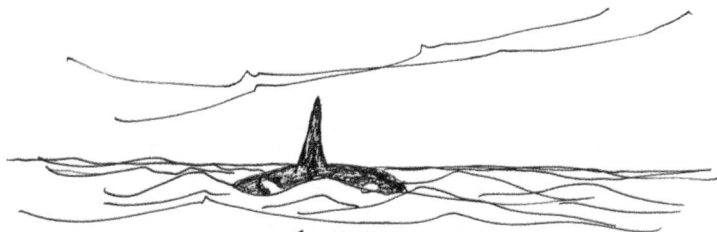

Killer Whale

For an hour next morning I tried to get us going again under the full sail, seven tall panels doing their best to squeeze some forward motion out of the merest caress of wind, but it was no good. A harbour porpoise crossed astern. I exited the hatch to check that all the nuts and bolts of the self-steering gear were still good and tight, and to squirt some more silicon spray down the rudder shaft. The fishing boat appeared again, hull down to the north, working its way east and west, and just after eleven in the morning a pod of killer whales, half a dozen or so, ranged round on the western horizon. The sun appeared.

Soon it was noon once again. We had covered just twenty-two miles since the day before.

Sometimes it can take hours for a calm to end as the wind plays tricks from every quarter, sending in tantalising but ultimately inconsequential puffs from here and there. This time it was different. The line of sea along the western horizon suddenly darkened, promising wind, and in it came, without pause or prevarication, a solid and consistent flow of air which soon had us slicing along nicely under the full sail. Every minute put more distance between us and our *nemesis* astern and so made me feel better in every way. We were getting on at last, churning our path through an adverse sea, throwing up a million bubbles in our wake, properly homeward bound once more. The wind veered to the north-west and so I eased off, sending us leaping forward, now under six panels and a brilliant sun. It was that kind of afternoon, the kind that swells the heart and thrills the soul, the kind that is perhaps the whole *raison d'être* of this sailing business; liberating, joyful, inexpressibly uplifting, totally *alive*.

The sunshine warmed the cabin and for the first time in weeks rid the portlights of their condensation. I could see clearly from inside the observation pod without having to wipe away a film of moisture that covered the windows. To celebrate this summery atmosphere I gave myself a complete refit: a change of clothes, a good wash, a shave and a beard trim. I even put a fresh pillow case on my pillow. I felt cleaner, lighter, somehow more airborne.

That evening we crossed 72°North. A sudden roar right beside the boat left a oval slick just a yard or two off our port beam, and a minute or two later several humpback whale spouts erupted astern. I wondered whether the whale which had surfaced so close had come in deliberately to have a look, or whether our encounter was no more than the intersection of two random trajectories. It was an important distinction. If the former, then the whale had timed and placed its surfacing with absolute precision, close enough for the best possible look at us without touching. If the latter, then it was a genuine near miss that, had either of the parties been displaced just a few feet in space and time, might have resulted in a serious collision. This whole question of collisions at sea was becoming one of the leitmotifs of the voyage. I was thinking about it more and more. The probabilities seemed to be stacked against it, but here was yet another close shave within a day or two of the incident with the buoys. I had calculated the chances of us hitting the buoys, a fixed hazard, at about seven thousand to one. I suspected that the chances of hitting a hazard moving permanently on the surface were the same, but the whale of course only surfaced occasionally. This must increase the odds against a collision massively. On the other hand there was more than one whale ranging about. The odds against hitting a specific whale were extremely high, but as for hitting *any* whale, well, maybe the probability was not as low as I may have imagined. Random collisions with whales had sunk many yachts over the years. I had neither the mathematical skill, nor enough data on whale numbers, to even begin to attempt any meaningful calculation on the odds of this happening.

Thinking about the chances of a collision with a whale naturally led to consideration of ships and fishing boats. These were permanently on the surface and much, much bigger. The big difference between ships and whales was of course the near-permanent visibility of the former. Added to that was human agency directed at all times, in theory anyway, at avoiding collisions. This human agency was harnessing technology more and more in order not to run into things. I was, by choice, a non-participant in this development. I could not be wholly sure whether this made me more vulnerable or not. Did reliance on myself rather than electrical circuits increase or reduce the probability that I would collide with a ship or fishing boat? The immediate common sense answer would be that the chances of collision were thereby increased. I was not so sure. The obvious answer is not necessarily the correct one. It seemed to me that it was as much a question of attitudes and behaviours as of technological hardware. The technology, on the face of it, is fine. It impacts, though, on behaviour, subtly changing it. A navigator bristling with radar and early warning systems and every up-to-the-minute gizmo feels confident and invulnerable, inducing him to relax his guard. The benefits of the former can be offset by the dangers of the latter, which is why even the best-equipped ships on the ocean still run into each other, or into shallows, rocks, islands, headlands and anything else available.

46

We had by now been at sea for forty days, a disparate crew of uncommunicative ragamuffins, somehow keeping the ship afloat and moving, somehow keeping body and soul together. For forty days we had evaded anything that might be termed heavy weather, but that was about to change.

A muscular north-westerly forced as down to one panel, veered to the north-north-east and began to wind itself up. With the breeze now on our port quarter we plunged on through light fog and rain, the familiar accompaniment to most of the voyage. As the night progressed the single panel was reduced to a half, and then a third, these reductions designed to keep us moving nicely but without griping up to windward in the increasingly heavy squalls. The third of a panel was finally reduced to just the sail bundle and at eight in the morning I lashed the bundle amidships so that we were, as they say, running under bare poles.

Our noon position gave us a latitude of 71° 19'North, so we had covered pretty much exactly ten degrees, six hundred nautical miles, since turning round to the west of Franz Josef Land. Our daily run was up to seventy-four miles, a good portion of that made under one panel or less.

The wind blew up more strongly but kept itself, just, within the range where we were able to keep running off. There is a fine line, when running, between neither going too fast nor too slowly, and between being under the full control of the self-steering gear and losing that control, the result of which is the boat tending to round up, putting herself at a more vulnerable orientation to the waves. In this instance the wind restricted itself to a healthy Force 7, perhaps just occasionally reaching a full gale in the gusts. Had it gone up another notch or two, threatening our ease and control, I might well have been tempted to heave-to, bringing us round to face the weather. Obviously I wanted to avoid this if possible, as we were making good progress on our ideal heading.

A big sea was building up astern and so I dogged down the main hatch and the aft portlight, completely sealing the cabin. For the first time on the voyage I decided that it might be better not to try cooking my evening meal; there was an outside chance that a panful of food might end up on the cabin sole. I opened a tin of spicy beans and a tin of mackerel, quickly mixed them up in the pan and ate the resultant mess straight off.

The rain came down more heavily; night became true night. I lashed myself to the leeward bunk, using webbing ties across my chest and thighs, and failed to get to sleep.

In total we ran for twenty-four hours under the lashed sail bundle, driven on by little more than the pressure of the wind on the bare mast. The waves rolled in from astern, sometimes curling into a welter of white water, sometimes passing under us with not so much as a splash. We dropped deep into the troughs and rose high onto the crests, descending and ascending to an endless rhythm. Night turned to yet another grey and rain-swept day.

We were approaching 70°North and the Cabin Boy, shifty-eyed and truculent as ever, emerged from somewhere deep in the fo'csle to demand his boiled sweet. *Of course not,* I said. *Not fair,* he replied. *We're nearly there. Why can't I have it now?* He kept his head down as he spoke, in his usual evasive manner, his eyes fixed somewhere around my left knee. I could see that with the voyage nearly done he fancied he could get a bit above himself. He needed putting in his place. *You can't have it now, you snivelling pimply wretch, because we have not yet crossed seventy north and no sweet is due until we have.* The little toe-rag wasn't having it: *But you know as well as I do that we'll be crossin' it in an hour or two. You and your stupid friggin' rules. I fancy a kip an' one of them glucose sweets helps me nod off. Don't make no difference whether I have it now or later, do it? Sick of all this bollocks in't I.* Well, this kind of talk was insubordinate, if not downright mutinous. It was time to exert my authority, an authority which honesty forces me to admit had declined somewhat since the episode with the exemplary array of buoys. *Listen to me, you lecherous little scumbag son of an illegitimate cabbage-grower, it is not a question of difference. It has nothing to do with now or later. It is a question of principle, a quality in which you are sadly lacking. It is about discipline, and more importantly, self-discipline. A pleasure deferred is a pleasure gained. It is about order. What sort of chaos would ensue if anyone could just help himself to a sweet any time he fancied it? Answer me that, you pathetic and grossly indolent, underachieving halfwit.* I was warming to my task. My leadership qualities were flourishing once more. I could sense that the rest of the crew, that execrable assemblage of also-rans, were now eavesdropping with wrapt attention, gleeful that the least of their number was daring to challenge their hated Skipper. I sensed too that this was perhaps a seminal moment. I had to rise above the common weal and show why it was I, and not they, who was Leader of the Expedition. I raised my voice a little, to be sure that every last man of them, wherever he may be secreted away, could hear my words loud and clear. *What you have to understand, you gangrenous little jockstrap, is that this world is not constructed solely for your personal gratification. Believe it or not, you putrid little worm, there are better things that you can aspire to. You want your sweet and you want it right now? Well then, you slimy nose-picking pile of gobshite, you can damn well learn to do without. No sweet for you until sixty-nine north! Yes! I mean it, you self-seeking swab of spittle. No sweet at all!*

Ha! That put them back in their boxes, every last one of the miserable riffraff. The silence in the nether regions of the boat was palpable as my pronouncement was absorbed and dissected. Yes, indeed. No sweet! That had given them something to think about. Sometimes a man has to show who is the boss.

47

We crossed 70°North and to mark the moment a patch of clear blue inserted itself into the clouds above, allowing that almost forgotten celestial body, the sun, a brief and welcome appearance. The wind was easing and we were sailing properly again. The half panel set just before nine in the morning was gradually increased to two panels by mid-afternoon. It was good to feel the boat pulling with more purpose; under bare poles there is always a certain slackness to the feel of the movement; a slight waywardness. I made a routine check of the bilge and was surprised to see a tiny residue of water down there. Perhaps one of the water bottles stored under the cabin sole had leaked a little, or perhaps it was an accumulation of condensation. For the first time ever on *Mingming II* I used the pump. Two strokes cleared the water. Nothing would appear again for the rest of the voyage.

The wind backed to the north-west and the sun disappeared behind an archetypal north-wind sky, a solid mosaic of regular and close-packed clouds. It was the sort of sky I knew well from these latitudes and one which often produced days of reliable wind. Instead it produced rain and another step change in the air temperature. I shed another top layer.

For the first time I began to sense the extra speed that our increasing lightness was generating. Forty-two days of food and water had been consumed and gone by the board, and *Mingming II,* relieved of that heavy burden, was starting to feel more responsive and frisky. We had now halved the distance between our northerly turning point and Whitehills. It was the thirteenth of August, and I allowed myself to start calculating possible arrival dates. This, I knew, was a risky business. In 2011, in *Mingming,* an intractable ridge of high pressure lodged in the Norwegian Sea had kept us more or less at a standstill for several weeks. Nonetheless I projected ahead, as sure as I could be that the northerly displacement of the Jetstream this summer would mean boisterous weather all the way home. Having crossed 69°North just before noon, and having therefore rewarded a sullen and unappreciative crew with the promised boiled sweet, I worked out that an arrival back at Whitehills on Saturday the twenty-fifth of August was not an unreasonable prospect. It meant averaging sixty nautical miles, one degree of latitude, per day to cover the remaining seven hundred and twenty miles. That, of course, was if we could sail a direct course, which was by no means a given. It was sixty miles a day against a current that would probably increase a little as we made our way south, until we were to the east of Shetland and into more tidal waters.

I raised another panel of the sail, metamorphosed by these calculations into a boy racer. It was time to get the old crate moving.

Within a few hours we were, of course, becalmed. Huge rain clouds revolved slowly around us, but their latent promise of wind remained unfulfilled. Nonetheless I could sense a change in the atmosphere. The stratified cloud we had grown accustomed to was making way for individual tower-blocks, white and expansive at the top, black at the base and letting off veils of precipitation. They spoke of the more confused and dynamic weather to come; unpredictable, squally, anarchic. We were at last moving out of the Arctic High and into the swirling systems generated by the Jetstream. It was time to take a deep breath before the real battle commenced.

I took advantage of this hiatus to rewire the solar panel controller, in effect linking the panel directly to the battery and thereby ensuring that as long as there was enough of a charge in the battery, I could use the navigation lights. I would have to be sparing in their use, but at least they were now once more available for moments of greatest need. Some years previously, in *Mingming,* when returning from the Davis Strait, west of Greenland, an expired battery had forced me to come through the Western Approaches and into Plymouth without lights. It was an unpleasant experience. I had felt both vulnerable and un-seamanlike and had no wish to repeat the exercise.

For a day or two we stuttered on as the weather tried to make up its mind. Torrential downpours scoured us from time to time. The breeze, as it settled in again, went round to the south-south-east, forcing us hard on to the wind. An adult gannet, the first harbinger of southern lands, escorted us boldly for a while. It rode the waves close to us and I would have liked to have photographed it, but rain intervened. The sky grew messier, mixing masses of threatening but indeterminate cloud with patches of moisture-streaked blue. We were approaching the Arctic Circle and I kept as strict a watch as I could manage; there always seem to be fishing boats hereabouts.

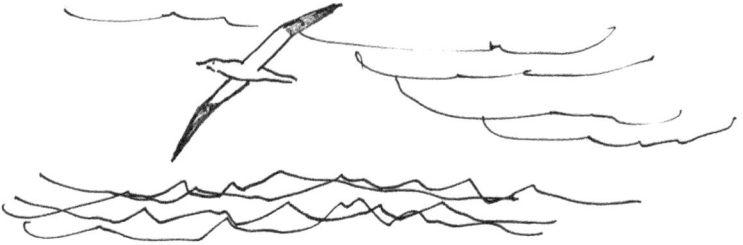

Gannet

At about four in the morning of Thursday the sixteenth of August, our forty-sixth day at sea, we left the Arctic. It ought perhaps to have been a momentous occasion, marked with a blast on the foghorn, but I was in fact asleep at the time. I wondered, on waking, whether I would ever return. Or was that it? Had desire run its course? After six northern voyages, more than a year's worth of uncompromising and unconditional sailing, had the compulsion been laid to rest? At that moment, I suspected that it had, but I also knew that I could never be sure. The need to venture once more into the wild places could re-assert itself at any time. It was a recurrent pathology that I doubted I would ever be fully rid of.

48

Then, at last, we were into the weather I had known awaited us. For a few days it had played a cat and mouse game, pawing us gently, sometimes leaving us alone entirely, taking its own sweet time before the definitive pounce.

I will not go through it hour by hour, or even day by day. We have to be getting on, after all, and while the fine detail of navigation can be absorbing at the time, it can lose its urgency in the retelling. I will paint instead a broad-brush picture of the seven or eight days spent traversing the band of stormy weather whirling through under the Jetstream. The ship's log is at my elbow, with every shift and change recorded faithfully, but now is the time to put that chronicle aside and delve straight into my memory for the impressions which live on.

I think first of the sky; so monumental, so confused, so dynamic. It was a sky of endless towering squalls lining up horizon to horizon; battalions of giant warriors packed shoulder to shoulder, their heads reaching up and up; huge engines of war, ever evolving and reinventing themselves in a constant expansive flux. Their low bases were as black as night and drove on vicious winds and biting rain. Sometimes the squalls were squeezed in so close one to another that there was nothing beneath them, end to end, but a solid and coal-black curtain of rain-filled gloom. These line squalls piled across from the west and the south-west in a relentless pouring, day after day. They meant that nothing was ever settled. Screaming squalls were interspersed with sudden lulls. The wind was forever veering and backing, just a few degrees each time, but enough to require a re-setting of the steering gear.

Squally Weather

Not far south of the Arctic Circle the weather worked itself up into its first real lather, a solid gale from the south-west. It was, in the main, a bright-skied gale, with piercing sunlight illuminating a seascape of self-assured wave-trains, rolling hills, hills rolling on, unimaginable weights of water heaving upwards and downwards in a regal procession. I stood up once in the hatchway and filmed the magnificence of it all, for such a sight is as beautiful as it is fearsome. I was not, in any case, afraid. I am past fear.

With the wind in the south-west driving on a huge sea, I was stymied as far as finding the ideal board was concerned. Port tack took us out to the west, but what with the wind and waves and the current we were being forced back northwards too, losing our hard-earned latitude. Starboard tack took us southwards, but also to the east, and there I had to be careful; too much easting would bring us into contact, eventually, with the Norwegian oil rigs. Moreover, we still had a way to go before reaching the Greenwich meridian, the ideal line to sail down to the east of the Shetlands. With this kind of weather from the south-west we were therefore locked into an impossible prison. All I could do was to hold position as best I could and wait for the wind shift that would release us.

In any case, whether we sailed this way or that was largely academic, as by now we were more or less hove to, forereaching gently under a fraction of the top panel. Hunkered snugly down, *Mingming II* eased along through the stupendous seas, as untroubled as ever. She was not always quiet, though. The heavier squalls would set the main halyard clattering against the mast. With very little sail set there was not much tension in the four-part haul, so a good gust would result in a prolonged burst of rat-tat-tatting as the halyard whipped back and forth against the upper part of the mast. It was a harsh, unwelcome accompaniment to the ambient sounds of the hissing sea.

Any wind approaching gale force also set up a moaning somewhere around the structure of the observation pod. I could never quite locate the source of this ghostly soughing. It was peculiar to *Mingming II*; *Mingming* had never moaned. As the wind increased it rose in pitch and intensity. Standing inside the cabin, with my head well within the observation pod, I could never hear it, but as soon as I lay on my bunk it started up again, a soft but penetrating and somewhat unnerving lament. It was a sound I grew to dislike intensely; for some reason it evoked a strong sense of aloneness and mortality.

After a day or two of trying this tack and then the other, and never finding a satisfactory heading, and of thus being forced to accept the status quo, the wind eased slightly and veered a little towards the west. Now I could harden back to our proper course, but we were of course now heading straight into a tumultuous left-over sea. I raised another panel of sail to give us more drive and we reared our way south, lurching through trough and crest in an ungainly gavotte.

The gale had eased but in the wider picture nothing else had changed. The squalls and overbearing lines of thunderheads marched in as relentlessly as before. Great curving tentacles of cirrus spread across the upper atmosphere, presaging more doom. For several days I appeared to dodge the worst. The southern edge of a system seemed to pass just astern. Another time I put in a long board to the west to skirt around another heart of darkness crossing ahead. I spent many hours trying to piece together the meteorology of the moment and so make sense of the confusion all around. It was a hopeless task, of course, but at the core of it lay a desire not to sail unthinkingly into the worst kind of trouble. In particular I wanted if possible to keep away from the north-east quadrant of any nastiness. The bare fact was that there was nothing I could do about it, given our slow rate of progress, but I still had to maintain maximum awareness, to keep analysing, to keep reviewing options.

There was the odd period of respite. For a short while the wind veered to the north-west and we raced to the south-south-west under three and sometimes even four panels, making up for lost time, clawing back our latitude. But the set of the wind was mainly from the south and so kept us always hard at work. Our compass heading and our actual course sailed were at a wild variance, what with the current against us, and the surface drift and the predominant wave trains. Nonetheless we were forcing our way south, degree by hard-won degree.

The sky closed in completely and the racing cloud lowered and lowered and I knew we were in for another merry time. The wind veered to the south-east and within an hour or two wound itself up to a fine old fury. It was a night-time blow in a night as black and opaque as a nun's habit. Half a panel was reduced to a quarter of a panel and finally any sail was too much. I stood up in the hatchway, scoured by the rain and spray driving horizontally across the wave-tops, and lashed the sail bundle as tightly as I could to the boom gallows, minimising any chance of movement or chafe. Bitter squalls screamed in, perhaps up to a Force 9 in the harder gusts. I sealed the cabin, lashed myself to the leeward bunk and escaped the tumult in uneasy sleep. *Mingming II's* moan became a wail, but it was no more than an acoustical trick, unnerving perhaps, and misleading too, for she was as solid and untroubled as ever in that heaving sea. With a ballast ratio of around fifty percent, a minimum of windage aloft with her unstayed mast, and her relatively shallow draft which allowed her to slip sideways rather than be tripped on a wave face, she rode the storm with regal ease. As the milky grey light of morning began to seep into the cabin, the wind veered to the south and then to the south-west, easing a little. I made a check of our position; we had been pushed four miles to the north-west, but now was the opportunity to make up the loss. I raised a panel and a half of the sail and set us on a southerly course. The seas were more confused than any we had met on the voyage so far, what with the combination of a severe gale and a quick rotation of the wind. We bucked and rolled our way southwards, thrown one way and the other as waves and swells competed in a right-angled tussle. By five-thirty in the morning the wind had veered a little further and so we were almost making our course despite the anarchic set of the sea. I increased sail to two panels to force us on through the chaos. It was a wild, plunging ride but I did not care. We were bound for home; my little ship was strong in body and firm of heart.

We were by now approaching 62°North, which meant that the idyll of a wide and open sea was drawing to a close. We would soon be meeting fishing boats and commercial traffic. Moreover, we were still hard-pressed to make enough westing to weather the mass of oil rigs still lying uncomfortable to our south. I treat an agglomeration of oil fields as if they were land, a huge island, and would never willingly sail amongst them. A mental picture of this land is created by simply connecting all the outermost rigs with an imaginary line. I treat this line with as much respect as if it were an actual coast. In the case of the oil fields to my south, this exercise created a north-west headland, the Magnus Rig. To its south-south-west, some twenty-five miles distant, lay the headland formed by the Tern Rig, with a shallow bay between the two, and due south of the Tern Rig, about twenty miles away, the final point to be weathered, the Heather Rig. After that the 'land' slopes rapidly away to the south-east and the Ninian Rig. My normal rule is to keep a good offing to the west of these outposts. I only once broke this convention, in 2011 in *Mingming*, when persistently calm weather gave me no choice but to cut inside the Tern Rig.

The wind backed, forcing us once more on to a course that would take us to leeward of the Magnus Oil Rig. That was an unacceptable proposition. I had no choice but to go about and head west in search of the Greenwich Meridian. With the sea now settled into the south-west and the North Atlantic Current on our weather bow it was a struggle to maintain our latitude; sometimes we gained a little to the south, sometimes we were pushed back north. It was the age-old story: patient manoeuvring to maintain the optimum position in readiness for the moment when a wind shift would release us from a provisional entrapment. Between the east coast of the northern Shetlands and the westernmost point of the oil rigs there is a passage about fifty miles wide. As near as was possible, I wanted to sail down the central line of that passage, thereby giving us maximum sea room from the hazards to our east and west. It was a simple precaution, deeply ingrained and unconditional, bred of the lee shore that had almost put paid to my life when I was barely more than a boy.

The sky cleared to a brilliant blue and a storm petrel flickered past. A ship crossed ahead, almost hull down and moving rapidly west. Whitehills lay less than three hundred miles away. The wind was coming off and I raised more sail, taking us to three panels then four, then five.

The liberation came rapidly and unexpectedly. Within the span of twenty seconds or so the wind veered sixty degrees, opening wide the iron-studded door which had kept us contained. I went about, raised another panel of sail, and there we were, ghosting easily south in a smoothing sea. Night fell and on we moved under a brilliant moon and a sky that sparkled with a thousand distant stars. I had forgotten the magic of night sailing in a warm and gentle breeze; the fusion with scale and eternity, the very strangeness of it all. I sat in the hatchway and lost myself to the sensuality of the moment, a rich amalgam of sight and sound and deep satisfaction. Every nerve end tingled. Aliveness and sentience were elevated to their proper scale. We take so much for granted.

Beautiful night became beautiful day. Under a trade wind sky and with all seven panels of the sail drawing her along, *Mingming II* danced easily through a benign sea. She was now light and agile, and I enhanced this further by jettisoning twenty litres of water. The Ship's Collector of Rain looked on in bemusement at this unspeakable sacrilege, but I had done my calculations and ignored his raised eyebrows and scarcely concealed sneer. Even with twenty litres consigned to the deep, we had enough water to last at least another six weeks. I had an urge now to enjoy the pure sailing qualities of the ship I had created. We had crossed nearly eight thousand miles of ocean together, but most of that had been in a dour cruising mode, with *Mingming II* too laden to have a chance to really sparkle. I knew how dazzlingly well she could sail from our stripped-out sailing trials, and now decided to give her a little more freedom to perform.

By noon on the twenty-fourth of August, our fifty-fourth day at sea, we were almost on the Greenwich Meridian. Over the previous twenty-four hours we had covered not much more than thirty nautical miles, but that was all to change: with a proper breeze coming in from the west, our newfound freedom to head due south, and *Mingming II's* increasing fleetness of foot, we were now racing. I could sense another change too: as we approached the eastern side of the Shetlands we were moving out of the influence of the North Atlantic Current. Liberated from that relentless counterflow, *Mingming II* leapt forward with a will. Under a brilliant sky dappled with airy cotton-wool clouds, I peered to the south-west. Somewhere there, hidden by the blinding sunlight, lay land.

At seven in the evening, as the sun moved round further to the west, I picked up the familiar bump and pimple of Unst, away on the starboard bow. We were seventeen days out from Bear island. It was the signal to reduce sail a little. For the whole afternoon I had been carrying four panels of the sail in what, for my normal cruising mode, would have been a two-panel wind. Now that we had made our landfall I could make the compromise between speed and comfort, and so reduced the sail to three panels.

Our arrival at Unst generated a rare moment of magnanimity on my part. I awarded the whole crew two sweets *simultaneously*, one for our crossing of 61°North, one for the sighting of land. The suspicion and disbelief of that seedy gang was palpable. *He must be up to something, don't you trust 'im an inch* was written broadly across their sullen faces. They unwrapped their sweets pretty damn quickly though, and stuffed then into their greedy mouths like kids at a birthday party. For five minutes all that could be heard were the smacking, sucking, slobbering sounds of a very private and self-satisfied gluttony.

49

Night fell amongst a welter of black rain squalls. The wind veered to the north-west, a perfect quarter, and I reduced sail to just two panels. *Mingming II* rushed friskily along, now light of body and unconstrained. The two of us, my ship and I, were by now fused as one. Man and machine, yes; animate and inanimate, yes; but what was she other than an extension of my own body, of my own will? She was the means I was unable to construct out of my own flesh, a short-circuit of the evolutionary process, in essence no different from the flint axe of a cave dweller, a tool, a key to new possibilities and, literally in this case, to new horizons. The voyage was a joint purpose, giving both of us equal meaning. Without someone to sail her, a yacht has no significance; without a yacht to sail, a sailor has no validity. The relationship between myself and *Mingming II* was therefore both necessary and complementary; each of us made sense of the other. After two months together, lived in a kind of profound intimacy and a totally mutual interdependence, the boundaries between one and the other had lost their delineation. We had not, of course, become a single entity, but sometimes it felt that way.

The remoteness of the seas we had crossed together had only enhanced the bond between us. In those distant waters she was all I had; we were lonely co-travellers in a strange world. As we came closer to the coast of Unst, and so began our reinsertion into a more pressing and mundane universe, elements of our harmony became more diffused. Ahead loomed the lights of fishing boats, four or five, horizon to horizon, all of them trawling in unfathomable patterns and promising the same old story: a long night without sleep. To add to the discomfort of the mix, bouts of wind-whipped rain were interspersed with sudden lulls, leaving us rolling and slatting until the breeze steadied once more.

We threaded our way through the maze of criss-crossing lights, trying always to keep one move ahead of their shenanigans. Once or twice they came too close for comfort, but with the wind now a good Force 5 from the north-west we had speed and options at our disposal, and so emerged into clear water unscathed. With the offshore wind settling in firmly under a clearing sky I set our course a little more to the west of south, directly for Whitehills, a course which would bring us past Shetland's westernmost point, the Out Skerries, just ten miles off.

I unpacked my two mobile telephones. The battery on my main phone had died completely, but the newer reserve phone had kept an almost full charge. I had many times noticed that for some reason it is possible to pick up a phone signal a good distance off the north-west Shetland coast. Sure enough, the phone showed some reception, albeit weak and intermittent. I decided to send two texts, one to Bertie Milne at Whitehills and one to Brenda in London, telling them I was off Shetland and expected to be in within a couple of days. I composed each text and waited for a good signal before pressing the send button. Both messages got away successfully.

I felt intensely relieved, knowing that after fifty-five days without any contact from me, without knowing where I was, or indeed without knowing whether I was still a fully-functioning organism, they could deduce that I was still alive and that the voyage had not been a total failure. I am the most fortunate of singlehanded sailors in that I have a partner who is neither a worrier nor a doom-monger. I have always been very clear with her that it is quite possible that I may set off and never come back. I have also been realistic about potential time scales. A projected voyage of sixty days could quite conceivably last a hundred days. So if I leave at the beginning of July, my usual assessment goes something like this:

If everything goes well expect me back towards the end of August; but if I am not back by the end of August, there is no necessary cause for concern. There are many, many factors which could slow me down, certainly by as much as another month at the least. So I may not be back until the end of September. If, however, I have not returned by the end of October, then, and only then, can you assume that I have met with an insurmountable and terminal problem. You can then open the black box file at the bottom my bookshelf, examine its contents, and live happily ever after.

The point which I have reinforced time and again is that small and engineless yachts on long voyages do not run to strict timetables, or indeed any kind of timetable, and that, in particular, the concept of being 'overdue' has little meaning. I will either get back when I get back, or not at all. Beyond that there is not much that can be said, and there is certainly no point in fretting about specific dates.

In talking about this aspect of voyaging with other sailors, this is the point at which the question of carrying some kind of tracking device usually arises. The argument in favour of having a tracker on board is more often than not made on the basis that 'your friends and loved ones can check that you are OK.' Implicit in this kind of statement is the somewhat insidious notion that not carrying a tracker suggests a lack of concern for the wellbeing of friends and loved ones.

There are two reasons why I do not make use of a tracking device. The first is simply that I am philosophically indisposed to being tracked. A tracker is not a neutral piece of equipment, like a compass or a barometer. It has a strong element of agency about it. It is not simply a tracker, but an *observer*. As such, it is a necessary participant in the conduct of a voyage. Physicists and philosophers have long told us that action is influenced by observation. In the case of a tracking device, I cannot see how it could be otherwise. If I knew that my every navigational move was being followed, I have no doubt that it would start to influence what I was doing. My view of my progress would increasingly be filtered through the eyes of the supposed observers; it would become a real-time performance for their benefit. To be tracked would in fact undermine the whole principle of the exercise, which is to enjoy a period of direct, unmediated and uncompromisingly solitary contact with the wildest places I can get to. There is no place in that concept for the constant intrusion of a kind of third eye.

The second objection to the use of a tracker is much more pragmatic. It is based on the question I have put many times to the advocates of tracking, and to which I have never yet received a clear and satisfactory answer. The question is this: *if for some reason the tracker fails, meaning that friends and loved ones are no longer getting position updates, what are they supposed to do? What instructions have you given them?* A tracker which is operating as it is supposed to may well give some reassurance to those following a voyage. The problem is that if the signal fails, the observers have no means of knowing why. Is the yacht in difficulty? Has it foundered? Or is it the result of a simple electrical failure? Do they initiate a search and rescue operation or do they just shrug and hope for the best? For a small yacht in a damp and salty environment the chances of electrical failure are very high. That may well be the cause of a loss of signal, but equally it may not. The failure of a tracking device is likely to cause much more anguish and difficulty than the absence of a tracking device on the first place. Let's say I had carried a tracker which had failed after three weeks, when we were off the north-west coast of Spitsbergen. The loss of the signal would have imposed thirty or forty days of uncertainty and worry, totally unnecessarily. Had I carried a tracker, my own instructions would have been unequivocal: *never, ever, under any circumstances, alert rescue services. Just wait. I will either be back, or I won't.*

The effect of a tracker is to draw followers into the daily progress of the voyage, to keep it at the forefront of their minds. I prefer the inverse: to be forgotten about for a while. To go off on a long voyage is a good lesson in one's own dispensability. Life ashore goes on regardless. One's own importance in the scheme of things is reduced to its appropriately insignificant proportions.

That may well be the case, but I was still unprepared for the reply I eventually received to my text to Brenda. I had kept my own message short and to the point, to be sure of getting it away in the weak and intermittent phone signal: *Hiya. Off Shetland. In from Monday on…xxx.* That seemed to me to cover all the relevant points – where I was, when I expected to arrive at Whitehills, plus a bit of partner-friendly kissy-kissy for good measure. It was, I thought, a masterpiece of precision, and I was looking forward to the reply, something, perhaps, along the lines of *OMG darling! That is wonderful! I have sooooo missed you!!! xxxxxxooooo!!!* A thousand variations on that theme coursed through my head as I waited for night to become morning and for the moment when I would pick up the next expected phone signal somewhere off the island of Bressay. Absence does indeed make the heart grow so much fonder. Just before seven I switched on my phone again. Sure enough, there was a signal and a notification that I had received a text. My heart flooded with warm and expectant feelings as I opened the message. This is what it said:

> *I don't know who you are. I think you have the wrong number/person.*

How many times, over the centuries, has a man gone away to sea and returned to find that the world as he knew it has changed? How many times has he come ashore after a long voyage to find that his wife has died, or moved in with another man, or that he has lost children he knew he had, or gained children he did not know he had? It is an age-old story. Such is the sailor's lot. The disconnection from the daily flow of terrestrial life can deliver many an unforeseen twist and turn.

Now I felt the power of that disconnection. *I do not know who you are.* Had I been away for so long that I had been forgotten? Somewhere in those Arctic wastes had I entered a time warp? Was the year still 2018, or were we now in 2118? And if she did not know who I was, could I be sure that I myself really knew who I was? For a few minutes I fell into a strange limbo, bereft of identity, uncertain of my assumed place in the world.

I sent back a brief clarification of *who I was: Roger.* There was, I admit, a temptation to embellish a little. Something along the lines of: *My name is Roger. Do you remember me? We have been together for nearly twenty years, as far as I am aware. I'm the one with the gap between his front teeth and not much hair, the one that goes off sailing now and again. A few months back I had a go at fixing the bathroom tap.*

I resisted the temptation. Maybe my original message had been too succinct. Maybe she was just being careful until she was sure it really was me.

It turned out that she had, in fact, been confused by the fact that the message had come from my new spare phone and so from an unknown number that did not show up as coming from me. Having cleared that up, I felt once more at ease with the world. An hour later a text came in from Bertie Milne at Whitehills confirming receipt of my message to him. He would be at the ready for further instructions.

50

Away to our west the undulating hills of Shetland rose above the crisply cut cliffs of Bressay. The wind was still a brisk north-westerly, setting up a boisterous sea although, given the short fetch to windward, the waves were now shorn of their pelagic majesty. We bustled along at a fine old pace, rolling down towards Sumburgh Head and Fair Isle and the old familiarities. Our noon position showed a daily run of nearly ninety miles.

Oil-ry Supply ship Torres Bressay

An oil rig supply ship made its way north a few miles inshore of us and not long afterwards a bright orange vessel, its colour a perfect match with that of *Mingming II's* wind vane, bore down on us from astern. Concerned that the ship might overrun us, I assembled the hand-held VHF radio and called her up. There was no response and I tried again. An answer came, but from an efficient lady at Shetland Coastguard, who had evidently picked up some of my message and thought it was the Coastguard I was calling. I was surprised that my radio signal had reached so far. By the time I had explained the situation the ship astern had altered course with a view to passing to starboard of us. She was the *Trans Dania*, with the helpful words SEA CARGO writ large on her topsides. A call finally came through from her, and a Nordic voice intoned a confirmatory *Ya, I haf seen you.*

Bressay from ESE c. 10 miles

By three in the afternoon, under a brilliant and lightly cloud-flecked sky, we had crossed 60°North, a 'big' latitude for both myself and the rest of the crew. That lamentable lot were growing restless; they wanted to be home, and another degree brought them that much closer. For once I felt a slight sympathy for them. They were a weak-willed, sleazy bunch, exquisitely antisocial and self-obsessed, but they had managed more than fifty days of close confinement with only the occasional flaring of friction. They had earned a run ashore.

Night was falling ever earlier and more darkly. The soft grey lump of Fair Isle, wide on our starboard bow, faded into a black night. Away on our starboard quarter a high red light somewhere above Sumburgh Head was the only remaining sign of land.

We were crossing the mouth of the Fair Isle Channel and I picked up two ship's lights square on our port beam. They were the two lights one prefers not to see, port and starboard, evenly balanced and rock steady. She was heading our way. I watched them for a little while and concluded that although she would probably pass a little way astern, it would be too close for comfort. Once more I assembled the VHF radio and called her up. Another quiet Nordic voice answered and I explained that I was a small yacht heading south-south-west a mile or so ahead of him. *OK. I will alter course.* The ship's starboard light flickered out of view as she eased slightly to the north to pass comfortably astern. *Mingming II's* rewired lights shone strongly and I hoped that my Norwegian counterpart was able to pick up our stern light and so confirm our position. I had left the radio switched on in case I needed to speak to him again, and so was able to eavesdrop the ship's conversation with Shetland Coastguard, taking him through the necessary questions and instructions to allow passage through the Channel. The ship was the *Gerd Knutsen* of the venerable Norwegian Knutsen Line, carrying, if I remember correctly, a crew of twenty-four and a cargo of 50,000 tonnes of some kind of treated water.

A fishing boat mooched around ahead of us, but well enough to starboard not to cause too much disruption. My store of green apples was reserved exclusively for finishing off my lunch, but at ten o'clock that evening I delved into the knapsack under the quarter deck, where they keep cool and fresh, pulled out a nice crisp Granny Smith and ate it whole, just like that. It was a disgraceful self-indulgence, but there were plenty of apples left, and with just a couple of days of sailing left, all being well, the lapse of discipline was justifiable. I raised the sail to five panels and hauled on the mainsheet to bring us hard on the wind as the breeze backed to west-south-west.

The morning twilight brought a sky spreading with high cirrus and for a while I thought that we might be in for a blow. That prospect reinforced the precariousness of the final approach to the Moray coast. In heavy weather it can be a hard, unwelcoming place, with no easy havens. The harbours ranged along the coastline are hewn out of an implacably rocky littoral. There are no bays in which a man can take refuge, no sheltering points, just a line of narrow man-made harbour entrances that no sane yachtsman would try to enter in an onshore gale. I watched the tentacles of cirrus curling ominously overhead and refused to be cowed. We would get what we would get, I would deal with it, and that was that.

The backing wind headed us for a while, pushing us to the east of our course, but the adversity was only temporary, for the wind continued its rotation. I went about onto port tack, and now under four panels, *Mingming II* sped fluently along, her head set directly for home. A three-masted staysail schooner passed some distance astern, heading south-east and motor-sailing, by the looks of it. My guess was it was on a day passage from Fair Isle to Peterhead or Aberdeen. I did the sums of how many sailing craft we had seen in the fifty-five days since leaving Whitehills. Three.

Just before midday we crossed 59°North, our penultimate line of latitude. I calculated that if nothing changed we would be in within forty-one hours; Whitehills was now just over ninety miles away. It was Sunday, so perhaps we would arrive around dawn on Tuesday.

Even though the tides hereabouts are not especially fast-flowing, their influence was now palpable, especially with the wind forward of the beam. The ebb caused a slight reluctance; the flood has us leaping forward. The wind backed a little more, allowing me to ease the sheet a fraction and ratchet up our speed. An incredibly long and very low ship passed a mile or so astern, heading south. By eight that evening we were due east of the Pentland Firth. Rain showers crossed from time to time.

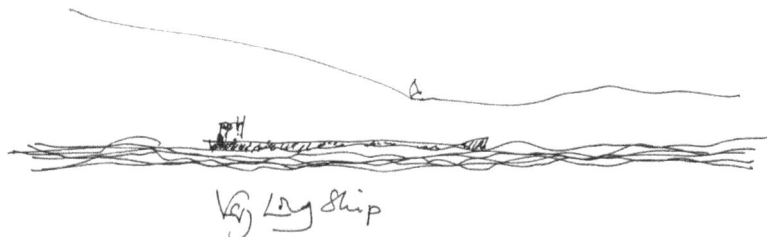

Very Long Ship

Just after ten o'clock, with the night now good and black, I became aware of lights astern, heading our way. It was a fishing boat, not trawling, judging by her lights and speed, but coming up quickly on a course identical to ours. I switched on our navigation lights, which I had been conserving for just this kind of situation, and watched her carefully. On she came, rapidly and relentlessly, a brightly lit and ugly brute, the noise of her engines filling the night air. Once again I loaded batteries into the VHF radio, screwed in the aerial, and tried to make contact. I called her up five or six times, but there was no reply. Was there anybody on the bridge? Was there anybody keeping any kind of watch? For all I knew she was careering along on autopilot while the crew slept or ate or attended to other things. I unhooked the self-steering gear and took over the tiller manually, in case I had to make a rapid manoeuvre. The fishing boat roared past on our starboard side, maybe a hundred yards away. To those unused to the sea, that may seem like a big margin, but in the wide ocean it felt like we were side by side, that feeling of proximity amplified by the darkness, which makes it difficult to judge the scale of a passing craft, and by the glare of the lights flooding her working area, which turned her into an industrial behemoth, and by the loud and hard-edged throbbing of her engines.

The fishing boat pulled away ahead, and I realised, with unnerving clarity, that my style of navigation had become an anachronism. I was out of time, out of place. It was a thought I had always resisted, believing that there was still a home for the simple seamanlike virtues based on human awareness. I now felt impelled to face up to the truth: the world had moved on; navigation had become an exercise in the alignment of electrical circuits, software, digital signals, binary algorithms, screens, automatic alarms and so on and so forth. The navigator was primarily a computer systems operator become seaborne. The pelagic world was now mediated through a filter of data streaming. Navigation was becoming a form of robotism.

Had I been so inclined, I could easily have adapted to all of this, but my resistance had been almost absolute. Was this unwillingness to change based on sheer bloody-mindedness, or a misplaced romanticism, or a strong nostalgia for my early sailing days, when navigation was still an ancient and largely unchanged art? There was perhaps an element of all of those in it, along with the strong belief that simplicity serves best. My sailing life had straddled the traditional and the digital, but as time goes on, sailors will only ever have known the latter. It was already the norm, and now I began to understand how out of step I had become. There was a fundamental misalignment between the practices and values aboard little *Mingming II* and the vast majority of vessels now plying the seaways. Put simply, I was yesterday's man.

51

The wind slowly eased and just before four in the morning I lowered the sail. Ahead, on the port bow, the several glows of the Captain Oil Field showed that we were on course for home. Whitehills was now just fifty-six miles away.

For an hour and a half we lay there, immobilised, but the interruption to our princely progress since reaching Shetland was short-lived. The night's rain cleared away and a steady breeze came up out of the west. I raised four panels of the sail and set *Mingming II* sailing full and bye, to give us a good clearance of the Captain Oil Field, and to steal a bit to windward should the wind back. My little ship bent to the task. We gambolled along in a smooth sea, making a good four knots, and I began to realise that we might be home by nightfall. This could be, with a little luck, our final run in. How fine that would be, to carry this soldier's wind all the way to Whitehills and so make port in one fluent board!

The Captain Oil Rig and her attendant ships passed abeam. I half expected another visit from a bright red RIB and an unsociable crew, but we were left alone. All morning we raced on. The sun came out and at two in the afternoon the Aberdeenshire hills rose above the southern horizon. Two Manx shearwaters, the only ones of the voyage, glided past on straight wings and a red and white helicopter flew overhead, making an infernal din. For ten hours we had been graced with as benign a wind as I could have dared anticipate, but the sailor's lot is never straightforward, and just after three o'clock the wind died almost completely. I raised the sail to six panels and then to seven, intent on wringing every last drop out of the fading breeze. To the north the sky was clear, and the edge of the high cloud cover was moving slowly our way, threatening, I suspected, an even greater loss of wind. By now the Moray coast was spread out ahead east to west. Was our smooth arrival home to be thwarted at the last hour?

A phone signal came in and I managed to get through to Bertie Milne at Whitehills. He pulled up the hour by hour forecast on his computer and gave me the bad news: at eight in the evening the wind would die to nothing, to be replaced by the lightest of southerlies. To make matters worse, we had arrived at the top of spring tides. The flood would soon be sweeping eastwards.

It seemed cruel that after the best part of four thousand miles of sailing, with our home port now literally within sight, there was a strong likelihood that we would be unable to cover the last twelve or thirteen miles before dark. The coast here is busy inshore, even at night, with the steady passage of fishing craft and creel boats. There was the prospect that I might be forced to move offshore again, to be clear of traffic and the worst of the tide.

Well, we still had a semblance of a breeze, and forecasts are often as not wrong as right. There was no choice but to keep going, to do what had to be done. Sometimes the wind strengthened a little, sometimes it died away almost to nothing, but *Mingming II* tracked steadily along, now showing herself at her best. The belt of cloud hung stubbornly along the coast, creating the final movement of air that would bring us home. The sea smoothed to an almost mirrored calm and *Mingming II* somehow conjured up effervescence and forward motion out of near stillness. The land came closer, yard by unrelenting yard. I could make out the Whitehills' harbour wall and behind and to its west, the white mass of Downie's fish factory. Somehow our progress through the water was maintained, on and on. The wind was now no more than the faintest breath, scarcely discernible at sea level, but up there at the masthead something was still drawing us along at two or three knots. By eight in the evening we were just four miles off. The tide was beginning to make more strongly and I pointed as high as I dared to keep our nose still heading for the harbour. The light began to fade. On we ghosted, still graced by the zephyr that now kept on beyond its allotted time. I washed and shaved, put on my favourite Faroese fisherman's sweater, and prepared a tow rope, going through all the rituals of a voyage's end, even though there was still no certainty that we would be in by nightfall. I spoke again to Bertie. He could see us from the bedroom window of his house, could see the tide setting us east. We agreed that I would call him again once I was a mile off.

Still we tracked on, but as we closed the coast the wind fell away still further. The lights of creel boats worked this way and that in the grainy twilight air. A boat with a bright searchlight came out of the harbour entrance and headed our way. We were less than two miles off, still moving, still striving for the last mile. The searchlight came closer and in the gloom I realised that it was a very bright headlamp. Beneath the lamp I could make out the distinctive turquoise hull of *Swee'Pea.* Bertie had decided not to wait for my call. He had rounded up his son-in-law Malcolm and here they were, circling around us so that I could pass the tow rope.

By ten in the evening of Monday the twenty-seventh of August, after fifty-six days at sea, we were safely berthed in Whitehills harbour. I made a final entry in the ship's logbook: *Voyage and voyaging over.*

Leaving Whitehills, view from windward. (Photo: Bertie Milne)

Leaving Whitehills, view from leeward. (Photo: Bertie Milne)

Passing the Captain Oil Field once again.

A Dutch superyacht heads for Lerwick.

A simple lunch of rye bread, butter and cheese.

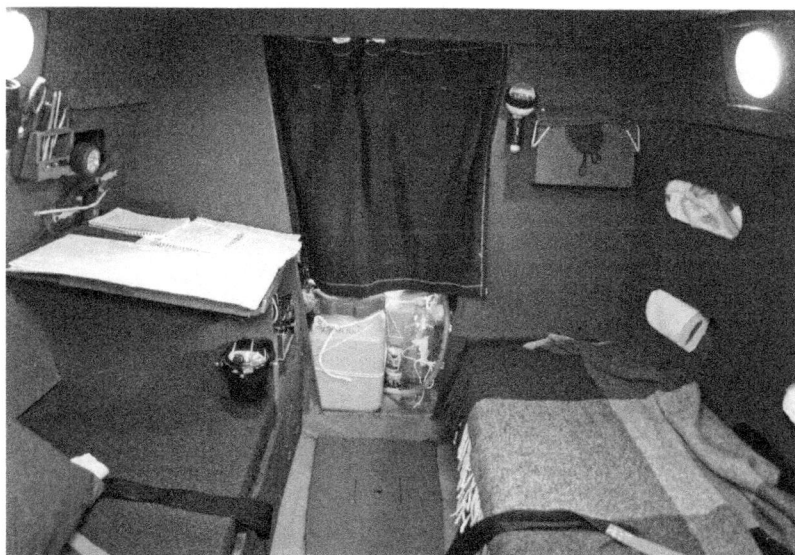

Mingming II's snug cabin.

The glaciers of Albert 1 Land.

A shaft of sunlight illuminates the Kaffitoppen.

A tame puffin examines us closely.

North-west Spitsbergen.

Approaching the Seven Islands.

Weathering Ross Island, with Little Table Island just to its south.

238

We leave the Seven Islands astern and head for Franz Josef Land.

The mother of all noon positions.

Iceblink over Kvitøya.

The Trans Dania passes close astern off Shetland.

Back in Whitehills after fifty-six days at sea.

One man's conception of the ideal pocket-cruiser.

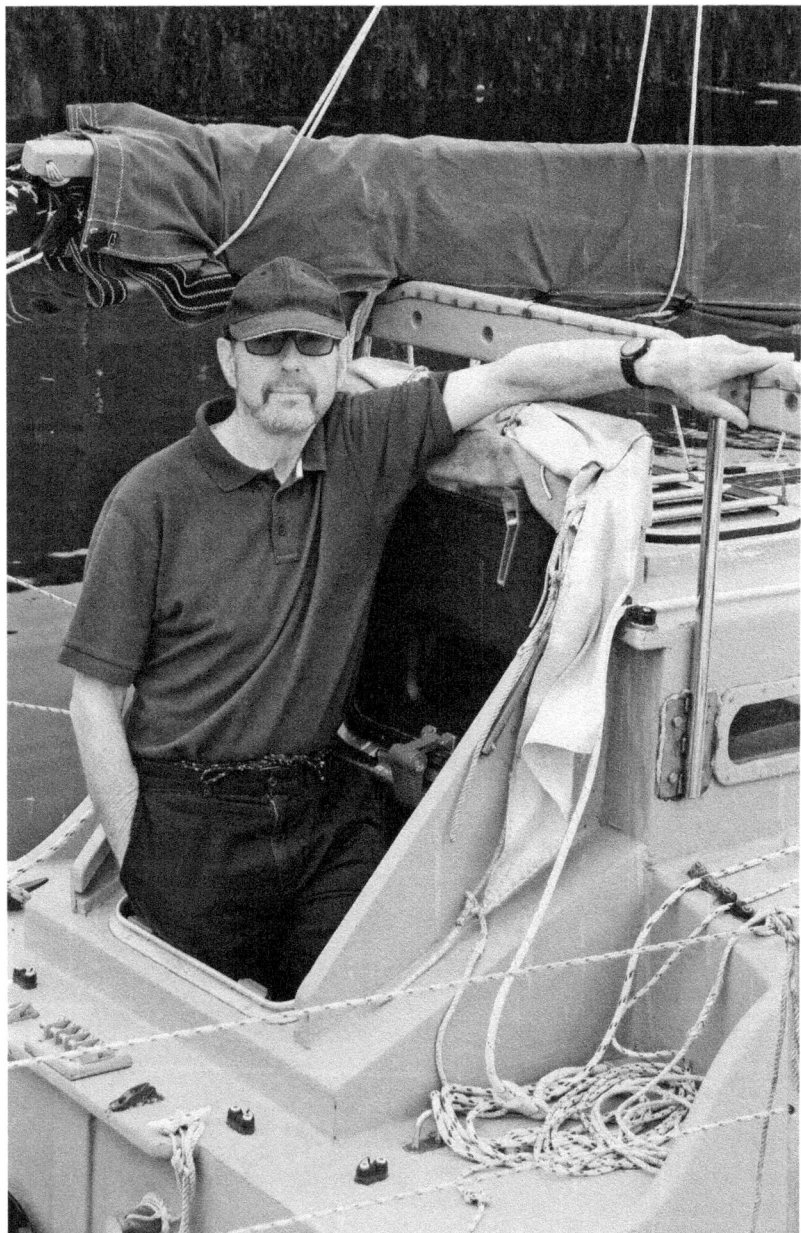

The author relaxes after the voyage. (Photo: Bertie Milne)

APPENDIX ONE

Statistical Analysis of *Mingming II*'s voyages

Voyage	2014	2018
Destination	Kong Karls Land	Franz Josef Land
Highest latitude reached	79°North	81°17'North
Days at sea	55	56
Distance sailed*	3332 miles	3480 miles
Average daily run	60 miles	61.6 miles
Highest daily run	97 miles	100 miles
Lowest daily run	13 miles	15 miles
Total sail area changes	309	322
Average daily sail area changes	5.6	5.75
Maximum daily sail area changes	17	12
Total exits from main hatch	17	7
Mandatory exits from main hatch	13	7
Discretionary exits from main hatch	4	0
Wet weather gear worn	2x	0x

* Total straight-line noon to noon distances. All distances in nautical miles.

APPENDIX TWO

Some interesting and relevant ice maps

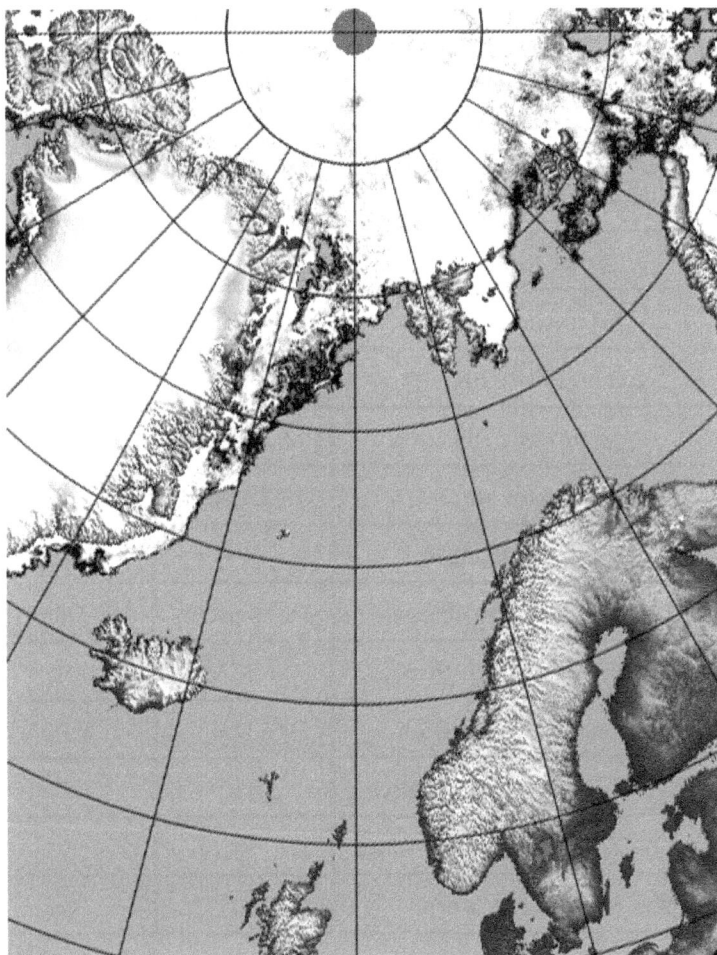

18ᵗʰ June 2017
*North and east Svalbard and the Queen Victoria Sea
totally icebound.*

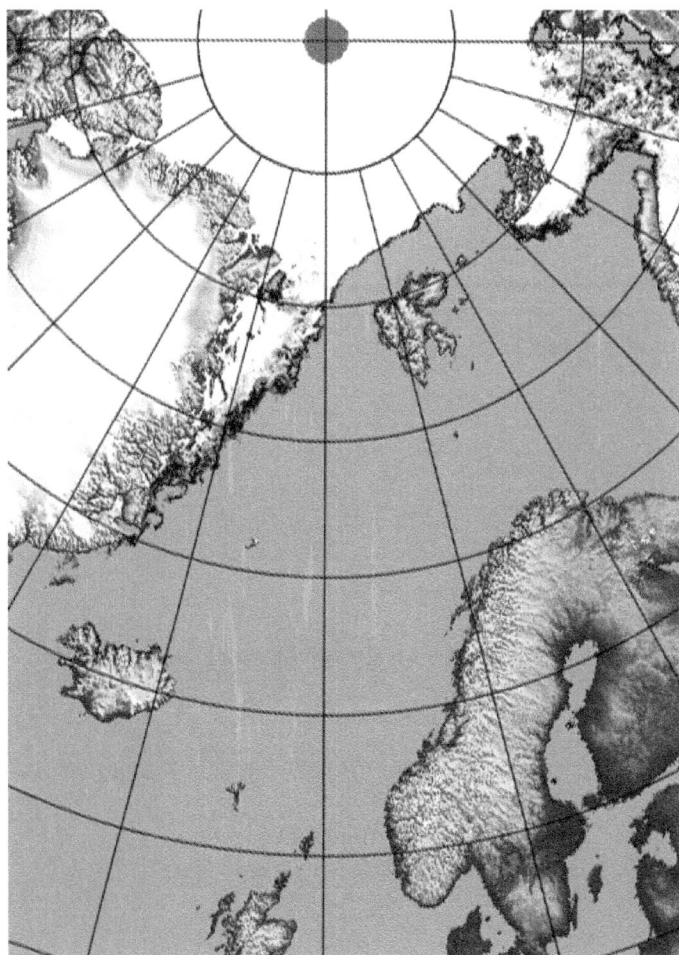

18th June 2018
*The whole of Svalbard and the Queen Victoria Sea
clear of ice.*

245

18th June 2019
Almost identical configuration to 18th June 2017.

11ᵗʰ August 2019
North coast of Svalbard still totally impassable and
the Queen Victoria Sea largely icebound.

Ice maps reproduced with the kind permission of Dr. Gunnar Spreen, Institute of Environmental Physics, University of Bremen, Germany.

APPENDIX THREE

MINGMING II – THE BARE FACTS

Under her remodelled exterior and new junk rig, *Mingming II* is a standard triple-keeled version of the Achilles 24. She is a derivation of the Oliver Lee designed half-decked racing keelboat, the Ajax 23. To create a cabin version, extra freeboard was added, increasing the overall length. The re-design was a joint effort between Lee and the long-time builder of the Achilles 24 fleet, Chris Butler. Fin and triple-keeled versions were produced. *Mingming II* is number 159 of about 600 built, and was moulded in 1980. Her principal dimensions are:

Length overall	23ft 9in
Length waterline	19ft 6in
Beam	7ft 1in
Draft	3ft 3in
Displacement	2600lbs
Ballast ratio	50%
Sail area	270sq. ft

The main sea-going renovations, modifications and additions are:

- Central keel dropped, sand-blasted, fibre-glassed, re-bedded
- Keel studs replaced
- Hull scraped back to gelcoat below waterline
- Topsides repainted
- Hull to deck joint strengthened with three layers fibreglass
- New rudder and tiller built

- Rudder tube replaced with solid 25mm stainless steel bar
- New rudder stock
- Rudder shoe strengthened
- Rudder skeg refurbished
- New floors and cabin sole
- Whale gusher double-action bilge pump fitted
- Two watertight collision bulkheads forward, compartments foam filled
- Watertight bulkhead aft, compartment foam-filled
- Lazarette sealed
- Interior gutted and completely rebuilt
- Hull and cabin top insulated with 25mm Plastazote foam, carpet lined.
- New fore-hatch structure built to take Houdini hatch
- Long cabin windows removed, replaced with laminated ply and two small port-lights each side
- Dog-house/observation pod added with central Houdini hatch
- Cabin extended aft, to create working Lewmar hatch and bridge deck
- Cockpit lockers sealed
- Series drogue bins built on cockpit seats
- Stainless steel series drogue chain-plates fitted to each quarter with 3 x12mm bolts and backing plates
- Foredeck strengthened
- Mast step and deck partners built for new un-stayed mast
- Hardwood blocks glued and through-bolted with 12mm eyebolts each side of mast flange to take halyard and parrel turning blocks
- Mast made from cut-down municipal lamp post, finished with nine coats epoxy paint
- Stainless steel masthead fitting designed and built
- New sail sewn, with laminated pine yard and boom, carbon fibre battens

- Boom gallows built and fitted
- All deck fittings removed and holes filled, or where kept re-bedded
- Canvas mast boot hand sewn
- Spray hood hand sewn for working hatch on copper tubing frame.
- Origo single burner alcohol stove under lifting chart table
- Hellamarine LED navlights powered by solar panel.
- Various boxes built for shelving, with sailcloth covers
- Pulpit removed, rope lifelines taken from aft to midships
- 10mm U-bolts spaced along decks for double harness attachment

APPENDIX FOUR

The etymology of the name *Mingming*

After buying the junk-rigged Corribee *Phaedra* in 2005, I set about the task of finding a more appropriate Chinese name for her. A very basic knowledge of Mandarin was a great help, as it is a tricky language, somewhat counterintuitive to the occidental mind. After a great deal of research I settled on the name *Mingming*. The word's meaning, usage, etymology and written form were perfect for my purposes.

The root word – *ming* – can be written in many ways and pronounced with different tones depending on its meaning (Chinese is full of monosyllabic homophones). The version here is written 明. It means 'very bright', and its ideogram is composed of 日 – 'ri' – the sun, and 月 – 'yue' – the moon (the idea being, no doubt, that when you have the sun and moon together you have the brightest sky). When combined to make two 'mings' it of course becomes 明明 – in effect sun/moon/sun/moon and is used adverbially – meaning 'very brightly, very clearly', but it is also used as a given name for both girls and boys (China's most famous basketball player is Sun Mingming – 孙明明).

As a navigator I found the idea of a name composed purely of suns and moons irresistible. Hence the sun and moon insignia on each side of the sails of both *Mingming* and *Mingming II*, which effectively give a pictorial representation of the yacht's name. The Chinese characters of course appear on my wind vane too.

ABOUT THE AUTHOR

Roger Taylor has been sailing small, engineless yachts to outlandish places for nearly fifty years. He is a recipient of the Ocean Cruising Club's Jester Medal, for 'an outstanding contribution to the art of single-handed ocean sailing', and the Royal Cruising Club's Medal for Seamanship, for 'achievements of legendary proportions'. He lives on a remote croft in north-west Scotland.